VOCABULARY IMPROVEMENT

Words Made Easy

Diana Bonet

A FIFTY-MINUTE™ SERIES BOOK

CRISP PUBLICATIONS, INC.
Menlo Park, California

VOCABULARY IMPROVEMENT
Words Made Easy

Diana Bonet

CREDITS:
Editor: **Tony Hicks**
Designer: **Carol Harris**
Typesetting: **ExecuStaff**
Cover Design: **Kathleen Gadway**
Artwork: **Ralph Mapson**

Copyright © 1992 Crisp Publications, Inc.
Printed in the United States of America by Bawden Printing Company

English language Crisp books are distributed worldwide. Our major international distributors include:

CANADA: Reid Publishing Ltd., Box 69559—109 Thomas St., Oakville, Ontario, Canada L6J 7R4. TEL: (905) 842-4428, FAX: (905) 842-9327

Raincoast Books Distribution Ltd., 112 East 3rd Avenue, Vancouver, British Columbia, Canada V5T 1C8. TEL: (604) 873-6581, FAX: (604) 874-2711

AUSTRALIA: Career Builders, P.O. Box 1051, Springwood, Brisbane, Queensland, Australia 4127. TEL: 841-1061, FAX: 841-1580

NEW ZEALAND: Career Builders, P.O. Box 571, Manurewa, Auckland, New Zealand. TEL: 266-5276, FAX: 266-4152

JAPAN: Phoenix Associates Co., Mizuho Bldg. 2-12-2, Kami Osaki, Shinagawa-Ku, Tokyo 141, Japan. TEL: 3-443-7231, FAX: 3-443-7640

Selected Crisp titles are also available in other languages. Contact International Rights Manager Suzanne Kelly at (415) 323-6100 for more information.

Library of Congress Catalog Card Number 91-76244
Bonet, Diana
Vocabulary Improvement
ISBN 1-56052-124-4

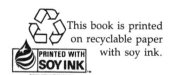

This book is printed on recyclable paper with soy ink.

PRINTED WITH SOY INK

To Gary and chocolate.

PREFACE

This is a book about words. It is especially for self-starters who want to improve their basic vocabulary and word-use skills. Some of you are learning English as a second language. Some found vocabulary study in English class boring. Now you have had a change of heart. Others want simply to reinforce your foundation of word skills by reviewing the basics. All of the words that you learn in this book are words that you should have in your vocabulary. You will know some of them already. Put a check mark by those you know and work on the ones you do not know.

How would you answer the following questions? If you must say "no," but would prefer to answer "yes," you are ready for this book:

- Do you know always which words to use when you speak or write?

- Can you express your ideas confidently and paint clear word pictures for others?

- Does your language express your real ideas, thoughts, and emotions?

- Do you "clam up" because you are self-conscious about your vocabulary?

- Are you worried that you will not use correct English?

By working through the exercises in this book you will gain confidence and move quickly toward building the vocabulary that you want. While you are studying, think of words as your hobby. Be curious about them. Become an expert at using them precisely. Spend time with them the way you would with a close friend. Each section teaches you about words from a different point of view.

Section 1 In this section, you will find answers to the important questions, "How can I improve my vocabulary, and why is it important?"

Section 2 Stroll through a fascinating history of the English language, from *thous* and *thees* to *DNA* and *killer bees.*

Section 3 You will get to know the dictionary as more than a doorstop. Learn to use this important reference book, and the thesaurus as well.

PREFACE (continued)

Section 4 Discover the secret of learning a thousand words at once, with prefixes, suffixes, and roots.

Section 5 Review fifty vocabulary words that you should know, with exercises for practice.

Section 6 Learn how Standard English and slang can exist comfortably in the same language.

Section 7 Play word games and build your ego, while you sharpen your vocabulary skills.

To learn new words, you will have to work a little. But gaining a new vocabulary is not as difficult as you might think. In fact, it is fun, and it has many rewards. A good vocabulary is an acquired skill, not a special gift. It is a skill that belongs to those who earn it. May this book help you do so.

Diana Bonet

INTRODUCTION

If you read this book we do *not* guarantee that you will become the president of your company. Nor can we promise that as your word skills increase you will marry a worshipful millionaire. What we do guarantee is that you and your vocabulary will be on excellent speaking terms. You will learn many new words and you will remember them longer. Vocabulary study is special because you learn to learn. By learning common word beginnings (prefixes), endings (suffixes), and roots (origins) you can learn not one, but a thousand words at a time. In no other subject can you achieve results so quickly.

Vocabulary Improvement is not meant to be read from cover to cover in one sitting. Check the table of contents and decide what chapter you want to work on today. Start there. Over several weeks you will cover most of the information. As a result of staying with it, you will benefit in the following ways:

- You will be better prepared for your high school equivalency exam, job placement test, or college entrance exam.

- You will improve your reading, writing, speaking, and listening vocabulary.

- You will think more clearly. Thoughts are limited by vocabulary.

- You will experience personal growth and greater confidence.

- You will understand other people's ideas and explanations more easily.

- You will gain important survival tools for the new millennium.

- Your friends will think you are getting very smart.

You will be happy to know that you already possess the tools that you need to learn new words. You learn new vocabulary from experience—reading, listening, repeating, using, associating, asking, linking, visualizing, rhyming, concentrating and desiring. By using the tools you already possess you will become a pro in no time. And who knows? Perhaps you *will* become the president of your company.

CONTENTS

Vocabulary Improvement

CONTENTS (continued)

YOUR VOCABULARY GOALS

Goals give you purpose and direction. They define what you want to achieve and provide satisfaction when you have achieved them. From the list below, check the goals that are important to you.

By completing this book I plan to:

☐ Add new words to my vocabulary

☐ Develop the habit of using a dictionary

☐ Use helpful, concise words when I write

☐ Express my ideas with clarity and focus when I speak

☐ Read more books, newspapers and magazines

SECTION

1

A Word to the Wise

CONTROLLING YOUR DESTINY

Primitive humans believed that if they knew the name of an object they could control it. Although we know that is not true, we do know that to possess a useful vocabulary is to control our own destiny. We relate to others with words. We express our thoughts and emotions with words. We convince, amuse and build trust with words. Words, and the way we use them, show age, income, where we grew up and how much we know. Words are tools. Imagine trying to pound a nail into a fence without a hammer. Imagine asking for a raise with a second-grade vocabulary. The right words give us control of our lives.

We live in a world of words. School textbooks and lectures expose us to hundreds of new words. Entering the business world forces us constantly to absorb new vocabulary and special terms (jargon). Job changes, even from one department to another, require that you learn more new words. Today, a limited vocabulary equals a limited chance for success. Most people stop learning and using new words by the age of twenty-five. However, successful people have a common trait. They have an in-depth knowledge of word meanings. They know how to use words correctly, and they continue to learn new words throughout their lives.

DON'T BE A WORD WIMP

Word wimps stick to the words they know. They play it safe for fear of sounding foolish or risking ridicule by trying new words. Here's good news. YOU DON'T NEED A BIG VOCABULARY! You need the *right* vocabulary. You can speak and write powerfully by using small words effectively. Albert Einstein used very simple language to express even the most complex ideas.

Are you a word wimp? If you answer "yes" to any of the following, this book can help you overcome your distrust of unfamiliar words and learn to use them to your advantage.

Do you avoid:

☐ Big words

☐ People with big vocabularies

☐ Newspapers, magazines and books

☐ Writing memos and reports

☐ Dictionaries

☐ Public speaking

☐ Thinking about your vocabulary

First you must believe that you can learn new words. Then you must want to improve. You need goals, desire, interest and a little time. Let this book be your guide. Improving your vocabulary may be easier than you think.

Actually, most of the 20,000 words that we recognize and use come from hearing or reading them in context. Context is the surrounding words in a sentence that provide clues to meaning. We absorb most words without conscious effort. Therefore, the easiest way to a better vocabulary is to read a great deal and participate in a lot of good talk.

OUR THREE VOCABULARIES

Here is something that might surprise you. You have not one, but three vocabularies. You have a vocabulary for reading and listening, one for writing, and another for speaking. Although they overlap considerably, each of these means of communication requires that we use our vocabularies in slightly different ways. Some forms of communication require larger vocabularies, *most* do not!

▶ **Reading and Listening.** These vocabularies include most of the big words that you know. When reading and listening, you notice words that you may not use yourself, but you recognize them by their context. When we hear or read new words often and find them useful, we frequently adopt them.

▶ **Writing.** This vocabulary requires simple words, organization and a knowledge of special terms within your organization—called business jargon. However, you should keep jargon to a minimum when you write. Always write to express rather than impress.

▶ **Speaking.** This vocabulary can be simple or sophisticated, depending on your audience. If you are speaking with your six-year-old nephew, little Freddy, speak simply. If you are speaking with technical wizards, use their vocabularies as much as possible. You should command the largest vocabulary possible, then adapt to your current situation.

A flexible vocabulary gives you options. You can communicate more effectively with a variety of people. If you are convinced that words are not merely interruptions in breathing, and you wish to pursue new words with vigor, review the following list of activities that build word power. Check those that apply to you.

CHECK YOUR ACTIVITIES

OUR THREE VOCABULARIES (continued)

In the past six weeks I have:

☐ Looked up a word in the dictionary

☐ Used a thesaurus (this is not a prehistoric reptile)

☐ Read a good book

☐ Learned a new word—on purpose

☐ Used my new word in a conversation

☐ Asked for a definition of a word I did not understand

☐ Completed a crossword puzzle

☐ Revised something I wrote

☐ Rhymed, repeated, or used flashcards to learn a new word

☐ Kept a word notebook

☐ Written a new word on my hand

☐ Played a word game

What other methods have you used to learn new words?

_____

_____

_____

_____

_____

_____

_____

REWARDS MAKE LEARNING WORTHWHILE

Since building a new vocabulary requires discipline, what are the rewards that make it worthwhile? Check those items with which you agree.

Learning new words can:

☐ Improve your chances for a promotion

☐ Allow you to communicate with many different people

☐ Increase your ability to learn

☐ Help you write more effectively

☐ Satisfy your curiosity

☐ Increase your understanding of the world around you

☐ Help you recognize words that others use

☐ Keep you safe

☐ Help you enjoy your hobbies and activities

☐ Enable you to speak to groups with confidence

☐ Help you pass your high school equivalency, college entrance, or master's degree examinations

Following are some tips to help you learn new words easily. As you review them, place a check mark next to those that you plan to use.

TIPS FOR LEARNING NEW WORDS

Here are some tips for learning new words. As you review them, place a check mark next to those that you plan to use.

☐ **Use new words.** Over and over. Choose a few words you want to learn, then bore everyone to tears. Use them in the office cafeteria, during meetings, while chatting with friends. Use them at the risk of making mistakes or appearing foolish. You must use them regularly to retain them. Count each time you use a new word. Try for fifty times in one week. By making new words a game, you will enjoy it more. Be sure that the words you select are useful to you and fit easily into your everyday vocabulary.

☐ **Carry a pocket dictionary.** You do not need the lap-breaker size to find most of the words you need; however, some pocket dictionaries are not always exact. You might want to verify the definition in a college dictionary later. Carrying a small dictionary in your purse or pocket allows you to look up words on the spot.

☐ **Use mnemonics (nih-MON-iks).** A mnemonic is a mental game to help you memorize words more easily. Acronyms and poems are examples. Remember the acronym for recalling the colors of the rainbow. ROY G BIV—red, orange, yellow, green, blue, indigo, violet; or the poem for remembering a spelling rule: *i* before *e*, except after *c*. Choose a word you want to remember, and associate it with something familiar or even naughty, or create a rhyme. Example: To spell the word *piece*, think of a piece of pie.

☐ **Write down new words.** Use a folded piece of paper as a bookmark and write down new words as you read. Keep a vocabulary notebook and add new words when you hear them. Check the dictionary for the correct spelling, definition and pronunciation. Use 3×5 note cards as flashcards, with the word you want to learn on one side and the definition on the other. Pull these out and practice them at odd moments.

☐ **Visualize.** Create crazy mental pictures of your word. Suppose you want to remember *anonymous* (meaning ''not named'' or ''unknown''). In your mind create a character with no face, named Anon A. Mess. Visualize his clothing as rumpled, with that freshly slept-in look (a mess). Exaggerate your image as much as possible. If you have to struggle a little to come up with a creative visualization, you will remember your word even better.

After reviewing these learning techniques, you can see that you have to work a little to learn new words. Thinking nice thoughts and swallowing little green vitamins will not improve your vocabulary. Learning new words is like dieting. You have to exercise your mind, choose your intake and stay focused.

S E C T I O N

2

Where Did All Those Words Come From?

IT'S ALL IN THE FAMILY

In this section you will discover the roots of the English language. To understand where our language came from is to understand more of ourselves. Every day the forces of language shape our relationships and our work. We live in a multicultural society, where language is sometimes a barrier. It does not have to be so. Most of us share a strong common bond, rooted in the Indo-European family of languages. Knowledge of our shared linguistic history creates the possibility of a broader point of view. A broader view creates tolerance, and tolerance opens the door to acceptance. Acceptance brings peace.

English is one of 1500 languages spoken by the 5 billion people on the planet Earth. One-half billion people speak English, although they may sometimes have difficulty understanding each other. Accents, dialects, tonal changes and occupations cause great differences, even within one language. Therefore, people from Atlanta, Georgia, may not easily be able to understand people from Cork, Ireland, or Auckland, New Zealand.

Nearly half of the world's population speaks one of the Indo-European group of languages. The English language came from this "parent" language spoken in Northern Europe about 5000 years ago. Eventually the Indo-European language family split and went into eight different directions. (Families had their problems even then.) Among the branches were the Celtic (now represented by Welsh and Irish); Hellenic (Greek); Italic (Latin and its children, French, Spanish, Portuguese); and Germanic (including German, Dutch—and English). These groups split and split again as words were lengthened, shortened, coined, swapped and dropped. The following words show evidence of the relationship of the Indo-European languages: English *mother*, German *mutter*, Swedish *moder*, Latin *mater*, Spanish *madre*, French *mère*; English *brother*, Dutch *broeder*, German *bruder*, Greek *phrater*, Sanskrit *bhrater*, Latin *frater*, Irish *braither*.

After a few more splits and splices, English began as an offshoot of the Germanic branch of the family. Specifically, it developed from Low German, named for the lowlands of the northern German areas where it began.

English as we know it has a short history compared to other languages. It is only 1500 years old. The development of English is divided into three periods:

1. Old English: AD 450–1150

2. Middle English: AD 1150–1500

3. Modern English: AD 1500–present

OLD ENGLISH: AD 450–1150

About AD 450 several Germanic tribes (the Angles, Saxons and Jutes) began to invade and conquer the island of Britain. Eventually these tribes occupied all of present-day England. These newcomers brought with them many closely related dialects (called Anglo-Saxon), out of which Old English developed. Old English also borrowed some words from Latin—the language of the Romans who invaded Britain around AD 43.

These were the foundations for today's modern English. The vocabulary of Old English was small. Approximately 85 percent of it is no longer in use. Most of the Old English vocabulary was replaced by French and Latin words. However, Old English was flexible and combined old words easily to form new ones. It was rich in prefixes and suffixes, so that old words could be changed for new ones.

Some words from everyday life are the same as they were in Old English— *cap, land, mat, meat, eat, fight, sleep, work, live, child, foot, house.* Some religious words were borrowed from Latin when Christianity was introduced in AD 597— *abbot, altar, candle, martyr, relic.*

Old English was also influenced by a 26-year Danish reign (1014–1040). Later the Angles, Saxons and Danes in England unified. From Old Norse spoken by the Danes, the English language acquired many *sk* words: *sky, bask, skirt, skill.* Some Old Norse words drove English words out of the language. If the Old English word for ''sky'' had prevailed, today we would be saying, ''Look at all of stars in the *welkin.*''

The Arab conquest of Spain in the eighth century brought many Arabic words into the European languages, including English. They were related mostly to science and math—such words as *alchemy, alkali, elixir, zenith, algebra* and *zero.* Some can be recognized by the definite article *al* (the) at the beginning of the English form.

MIDDLE ENGLISH: AD 1150–1500

Middle English developed from Old English, with heavy borrowing from French. There was also some borrowing from Latin. Sometimes three words of different origins meant almost the same thing: *ask* (from Old English); *question* (from French); and *interrogate* (from Latin). Middle English was the earliest form of the language that was clearly English. Modern-day English speakers can read Middle English texts without too much difficulty—for example, Geoffrey Chaucer's *Canterbury Tales*. Middle English was not yet an individual language, but a group of dialects not yet standardized. However, due to the Norman conquest in 1066, Middle English was not the primary language in England. The French language dominated England until the beginning of the Renaissance, around 1400.

About ten thousand loanwords entered the language in the Middle English period. Loanwords are words borrowed from other languages. *Justice* is a loanword from French that has become part of the English language. About 75 percent of the French loanwords from the Norman conquest are still used in some form today. In the Middle English period, French became the language of the court and the upper classes. Although the common people and middle classes still spoke English, French changed almost every aspect of the English vocabulary, and more of the Old English elements dropped out of the language. Some French loanwords include:

Topic	Borrowed Words
government	realm, royal, govern, mayor
social rank	prince, duchess, baron, peasant
law	justice, suit, jury, pardon
religion	saint, mercy, charity, preach
defense	war, peace, battle, lieutenant
wearing apparel	costume, robe, cape, lace, jewel
food	beef, gravy, cream, peach, jelly, vinegar, spice, mince, roast

MIDDLE ENGLISH: AD 1150–1500 (continued)

French influence greatly simplified the English vocabulary by changing the forms of many verbs. Old English had a lot of "strong verbs," such as *sing, sang, sung*. The French changed many verbs to "weak verbs" with *-ed* endings, such as *talk, talked*. Some modern-day verbs have retained their strong forms, such as *drink, drank, drunk; swim, swam, swum*. When English and French words were both used, their meanings gradually changed. Today we have the following words that were originally the same in meaning.

English	French
doom	judgment
hearty	cordial
sheep	mutton
swine	pork
calf	veal
house	mansion
ask	demand

Even after the year 1200 when France lost its power in England, French remained the dominant language.

In the Middle Ages, Latin was the language of universities, law and official documents. Many words came into English directly from Latin, such as *adjacent, genius, index, inferior, intellect, lucrative, limbo, minor, necessary*. Greek words came in through Latin and French, many as technical terms introduced by educated people: *scepter, theology, schism, heresy*.

Over time, a growth of national pride led to a reclaiming of the English language. Around the fourteenth century, English again became the language of the upper class (nobility), the law courts and the schools. Although English was well established during this period, many felt that Latin should be restored as the language of learning. They said English was *gross*. (Thus, *gross* was not a word created by modern teenagers.) However, these arguments were drowned out by the public demand for English translations of foreign books and articles. Toward the end of the fourteenth century the invention of the printing press sped the emergence of a standard written language. The standard English in the sixteenth century was based largely on the dialect of the populous district of the East Midlands. Oxford, Cambridge, Westminster and London were located there. This was the language of Chaucer's tales. Gradually the language developed into Modern English.

MODERN ENGLISH:
AD 1500 TO THE PRESENT

The sixteenth and seventeenth centuries added thousands of new words to the language, most of them from Latin. Modern English probably owes more of its vocabulary to Latin than to any other language. English also borrowed from Greek, either directly or via Latin. French, Italian, Portuguese and Spanish also contributed. Early dictionaries appeared during this time. You may have heard the phrase ''Neither a borrower nor a lender be.'' If we followed that principle strictly, the English language would be very different from what it is today.

Modern English developed rapidly as a result of the Renaissance. The theater, printed materials, education, booming business and social awareness created a stimulating setting for the language. As English developed, its pronunciation changed so that it became more like we hear it today. It continued to borrow heavily from other languages to meet the demands for words to describe new activities and new knowledge. New words entered the language at a rapid rate as England traded with the Low Countries and with northern Germany, especially in wool. Dutch, Flemish and Low German words entered the language: *yacht, schooner, sloop, cruise, skipper, mate, swab, deck, freight, smuggle* and *dollar. Measles, pickle, plump, poppycock, slurp, snoop* and *sputter* were added. As the British empire expanded in the eighteenth century, so did its vocabulary. From the American Indians were borrowed the words *caribou, hominy* and *moose.* From Spain came *chocolate,* for which we are all grateful. Great Britain built a vast empire in North America, India and Australia, thus expanding English throughout the world. Hindi, a language of India, contributed *jungle* and *thug.* Australia gave us *boomerang,* a word that comes and goes. American English advanced new words to fill the needs of colonial life, such as *bullfrog, sidewalk, cent* (coined by Thomas Jefferson around 1785).

The earlier creativity of the Renaissance began to give way to the need for order. People wanted an organized system that would conform to a standard. Attempts to standardize the language resulted in style manuals, grammar books and Dr. Samuel Johnson's *Dictionary of the English Language* (1755).

From the Industrial Revolution to the advancing technology of today, English-speaking people have created new words to meet their ever-changing needs. Words such as *manufacturing, automobile, telephone, computer, television, relativity, evolution, automation, stethoscope, psychoanalysis, countdown, astronaut, caller ID* and *global warming* reflect the energy and dynamic growth of the English language.

ENGLISH TODAY

Of all European languages, English has the simplest grammar. It is an analytic language, which means that it shows the relationship of words by their positions in a sentence, and by the use of prepositions. In English, a noun is usually followed by a verb, then a direct object. These words are linked by modifiers such as adjectives and prepositional phrases. Most of the time. For all of its assets, English has two serious problems. First, it is full of idioms. Idioms are expressions that vary from the grammar rules or from the usual dictionary meaning. They are unexpected word detours that make no sense unless you know what they mean. A *snap* is an easy task; *to get the brushoff* is to be ignored or dismissed; and *to get cold feet* is to lose confidence.

Additionally, English spelling is a mess! We represent the same sound in several different ways. Note how the *sh* sound is represented in *sugar*, *tension*, *tissue*, *fission*, *motion*, *ocean*, *suspicion*, *nauseous*, *conscious* and *shin*.

English-speaking students struggle to speak and write correctly, and those who learn English as a second language find the task very difficult indeed. For all of its simple construction and its wide range of vocabulary, English is perhaps too complicated ever to be adopted as a world language.

Exercise for Practice

In the following exercise, match the loanword in the left column with its origin in the right column. All of the words are mentioned in this chapter. Check your answers at the bottom of the page.

	Loanword		Origin
1. _____	bask	a.	Colonial American
2. _____	realm	b.	Old English
3. _____	genius	c.	Latin
4. _____	moose	d.	Arabic
5. _____	fight	e.	Spanish
6. _____	yacht	f.	Dutch
7. _____	zenith	g.	American Indian
8. _____	jungle	h.	Old Norse
9. _____	sidewalk	i.	Hindi
10. _____	chocolate	j.	French

Answers: 1 h, 2 j, 3 c, 4 g, 5 b, 6 f, 7 d, 8 i, 9 a, 10 e

3

Digging the Dictionary

WHAT A BOOK!
IT'S GOT **EVERYTHING**:

ro-mance´
ad-ven´ture
in-trigue´
com´e-dy
pa´thos
sus-pense´
pas´sion
dra´ma
vi´o-lence
et cet´era

WHAT'S IN A DICTIONARY?

> **dic·tio·nary** \ˈdĭk-shə-nĕrˈ-ē\ *n:* a reference book containing a selection of words usually listed in alphabetical order, with information about their meanings, pronunciations, and histories.

If you plan to learn new words, you will want to become friends with your dictionary. It is the most useful word book you can own. It tells you what a word means and how many different meanings it has. You can check spelling, pronunciation and parts of speech. You will learn where to break (hyphenate) a word when you have too little right margin to complete the word on the same line. It tells you what words are capitalized, how they are used, their histories and what other words have the same meanings (synonyms) or opposite meanings (antonyms). Depending on the size (and weight) of your dictionary, it may tell you much more.

What Dictionary Should You Use?

Dictionaries come in paperbacks, desk copies, simplified versions for elementary schools and college editions. The most famous is the *Oxford English Dictionary* (the OED), published in England. It is an unabridged dictionary, meaning that it includes all words and all definitions for each word. Experts consider it the most complete dictionary in the world. The newest edition of the OED has twenty volumes and 22,000 pages.

Your dictionary will serve you often and influence you more than all other reference books combined. When buying a dictionary, look for a convenient size and buy one that is easy to understand. Several good dictionaries are the *Random House College Dictionary, Funk and Wagnall's New Standard Dictionary* (unabridged), *The American Heritage Dictionary* (paperback), and *Webster's College Dictionary*. Visit your favorite book store or library and ask for a recommendation. Often you can find just the right dictionary in a second-hand book store at a low price. At any price, a good dictionary is a bargain.

WHAT'S IN A DICTIONARY? (continued)

Exercise #1 for Practice

Which of the following items of information can you find in a dictionary? Write "yes" or "no" next to each item. Refer to your dictionary if you are not sure of the answers. You may have to look in more than one dictionary to find this information. When you have finished, check your answers at the end of this section.

1. _____ the meaning of *biochip*
2. _____ where to break the word *gravity*
3. _____ your grandmother's address
4. _____ where the word *gem* originated
5. _____ an opposite word for *slow*
6. _____ ten meanings for the word *right*
7. _____ number of syllables in *lambada*
8. _____ who are Tom, Dick and Harry?
9. _____ how to fix your stereo
10. _____ is *muskrat* a noun
11. _____ the current weather in Japan
12. _____ how to pronounce *suite*

Facts About the Dictionary

► The first English dictionary was published in 1449.

► Noah Webster wrote the first American dictionary. He worked twenty years to complete his project. His dictionary defined 70,000 words. (Today's large unabridged dictionaries define several million words.)

► Words are placed in the dictionary when they appear often enough in printed material to gain general public acceptance.

► Words do not have to be "proper English" to appear in the dictionary. Slang is also defined.

USING THE DICTIONARY LESS AND ENJOYING IT MORE

Each time you open your dictionary, grab a new word and make it your own. Repeat it, spell it, try it on your mother-in-law. Soon you will know many new words and you will not have to refer to your dictionary as often. When you do, however, you will enjoy the chance to learn new words and gain more insight into words you already know.

To help you use the dictionary less, you should know how it is organized.

All entries (words) are arranged in alphabetical order. You can find entries quickly by using the guide words printed at the top of each page. The guide word on the left is the first word on that page; the guide word on the right is the last word on that page. By looking at the guide words, you decide if the word you want comes between these two words in the alphabet. For example, you would find the word *plain* on a page that had *place* and *planet* as the guide words, because *plain* comes after *place* and before *planet*. However, if you were looking for *plant* you would have to turn to the next page, because *plant* comes after *planet* when the words appear in alphabetical order.

Exercise #2 for Practice

Put the following words in alphabetical order in the spaces below. When you have finished, check the end of this section for the answers.

sad	grape	flake
brace	bloomers	mustard

1. _____   4. _____

2. _____   5. _____

3. _____   6. _____

If the first letters of two words are the same, you must go to the second letter to put the words in correct order. For example, *every* would appear before *extra* because the letter *v* appears before the letter *x* in the alphabet.

USING THE DICTIONARY LESS AND ENJOYING IT MORE (continued)

Exercise #3 for Practice

Put the following words in alphabetical order in the spaces below. You can check your answers at the end of this section when you have completed the exercise.

city	cent	cape
credit	consult	cute

1. _____ 4. _____

2. _____ 5. _____

3. _____ 6. _____

If the first *two* letters of two or more words are the same, you must go to the third letter to place the words in correct alphabetical order. If the third letters are the same you must go to the fourth letter, and so on.

Exercise #4 for Practice

Put the following words in alphabetical order in the spaces below. Check your answers at the end of the section.

when	what	whom
why	where	while

1. _____ 4. _____

2. _____ 5. _____

3. _____ 6. _____

In these exercises you practiced alphabetizing words that begin with the same letters. When words begin with the same letters, simply go on to the next letter. At times you may have to go as far as eight or more letters in order to place words in the right order.

Exercise #5 for Practice

Put the following words in alphabetical order in the spaces below. Check your answers at the end of this section.

sense	sensation	sentence
sensor	sensitive	senate

1. _____   4. _____

2. _____   5. _____

3. _____   6. _____

Look at these two words: *hat* and *hate*. Which word comes first in the dictionary? The answer is *hat*, because it has fewer letters than *hate*. The word with fewer letters always comes first. Thus, *to* comes before *too*, and *too* comes before *took*.

Exercise #6 for Practice

Place the following words in alphabetical order in the spaces below. Check your answers at the end of this section.

investment	invest	in
invert	invent	invoke

1. _____   4. _____

2. _____   5. _____

3. _____   6. _____

USING THE DICTIONARY LESS AND ENJOYING IT MORE (continued)

Exercise #7 for Practice

Here is a longer list of words to arrange in alphabetical order.

macaroni	whimper	shrimp
cute	shrub	wiggle
where	anteater	wimp
jingle	mussel	dangle
social	cut	muscle
socialize	must	wig
ant	jiggle	

1. _____

2. _____

3. _____

4. _____

5. _____

6. _____

7. _____

8. _____

9. _____

10. _____

11. _____

12. _____

13. _____

14. _____

15. _____

16. _____

17. _____

18. _____

19. _____

20. _____

In the next exercise you will be working with guide words. These are the words printed at the top of each page in the dictionary that tell you the first and last words on that page.

Exercise #8 for Practice

In this exercise you will see a pair of guide words on the left and a list of words on the right. First, underline the words on the list at the right that would appear on a page in the dictionary that has as its guide words the two words listed on the left. Next, list the correct words in alphabetical order in the spaces below the guide words. (NOTE: Six spaces are provided for each set of guide words. However, the number of correct answers may vary from one to six.)

Example

Guide words:

grasp to *grave* (a) Underline the words that come between *grasp* and *grave*:

<u>grape</u>, <u>grass</u>, <u>grateful</u>, graph, gravel, <u>gratify</u>

(b) Then list the underlined words in alphabetical order:

grass	gratify	
grateful		

Now do the same for these:

main to *make*	mall, major, mainly, maize, making, maintain

lag to *lamb*	leg, lagoon, lake, lamp, laid, lack

boss to *bowl*	bow, born, about, bowling, bound, both

FINDING GOLD IN THE DICTIONARY

Now you can find "gold" in your dictionary. (It is between the guide words *goggle-eyed* and *gold miner* in the newest *Webster's College Dictionary*.) You may want to know what other treasures of information your dictionary provides. It provides far more than an alphabetized list of words. First, the front pages tell you how to use your dictionary. Then it directs you to such useful information as pronunciations of common foreign words and phrases; population figures; lists of signs and symbols and what they represent; information about famous people; and geographical information. The most important part of the dictionary is its word entries. Word entries are the individual words your dictionary defines, in alphabetical order. In the remainder of this chapter you will learn the wealth of information you will find with each word entry. By working through the practice exercises you will increase your skills at digging out such important information as:

- Definitions

- Spelling

- Number of syllables (syllabication)

- Pronunciation

- Part of speech

- History (etymology)

- Synonyms (words similar in meaning) and antonyms (words opposite in meaning).

DEFINITIONS

A good dictionary gives you a concise definition of a word you wish to find. However, many words have more than one meaning, so you must decide which meaning you need. The context (how the word is used in a sentence) helps you decide which definition you need. If you are familiar with parts of speech (nouns, verbs, adjectives, etc.) you can find the correct meaning by looking up the noun meaning or the verb meaning, depending on the one you need. You must consider both the dictionary definition and the meaning of the whole sentence when deciding which definition to use.

Example: When the word *hand* is used as a noun it can mean the thing with the fingers at the end of your arm; or it can mean a hired worker. Be sure to consider both context and parts of speech when determining the definition you want.

Exercise #9 for Practice

Find in your dictionary the correct meaning of the italicized word in each sentence below. Write the meaning in the space provided. Check your answers at the end of the section.

1. Midwestern farmers raise wheat, corn and other *grains*.

   _____

2. A few *grains* of sand in your tennis shoes soon feel like boulders.

   _____

3. If you apply a walnut stain to the desk, the *grain* will show more clearly.

   _____

4. Hosea's babbling was so confusing he did not make a *grain* of sense.

   _____

5. Each tablet contained 5 *grains* of sedative.

   _____

6. Henry worked his way through college by *pitching* hay during the summers.

   _____

7. Trudy had always wanted a house with a *pitched* roof.

   _____

8. When the storm approached we decided to *pitch* our tents in a sheltered cove.

   _____

9. If you would *pitch* in some money, we could buy a pizza.

   _____

10. Our sailboat *pitched* dangerously in the wild seas.

    _____

FINDING GOLD IN THE DICTIONARY (continued)

SPELLING

''How can I check the spelling of a word in the dictionary when I don't know how to spell the word?'' Good question. First, the dictionary is the best place to find the correct spelling of a word. It gives the most accepted spelling for any word listed, and an alternate spelling if there are two possible spellings. Next, you can find the correct spelling by figuring out the first letters of the problem word. Here are some tricks to help you determine the first letters of a word:

- If a word sounds like it begins with *s* but you cannot find it in the *S* section, look under *c* (cent, cell) or *ps* (psychic, psalm).

- If a word sounds like it begins with *f* but it does not, try *ph* (phone, photograph).

- If a word sounds like it begins with *r* and you cannot find it, try *wr* (write, wrong).

- If a word sounds like it begins with *n* but does not, try *gn* (gnome, gnat), *kn* (knife, knee), *pn* (pneumonia) or *en* (enrage, end).

- If a word sounds like it begins with *k* but it does not, try *c* (click, claim).

- If a word sounds like it begins with *j* and you cannot find it, try *g* (gym, germ).

- If a word sounds like it begins with *o* but does not, try *en* (entree, encore).

Exercise #10 for Practice

In the spaces provided, list the letters you could check in the dictionary to find the correct spelling for words that sound the same as these. When you complete the exercise check your answers at the end of the section.

1. fraze _____
2. sykidelik _____
3. onvelope _____
4. nok _____
5. sikology _____
6. fotograf _____
7. jenius _____
8. klaim _____
9. rek _____
10. jentle _____

SYLLABLES

In normal speech, words are pronounced in a continuous flow, not as separate syllables. A syllable is a single unit of sound. *House* is one syllable because it is one sound. *Doghouse* is two syllables because it has two sounds. Your dictionary divides words into syllables so that you can more easily sound out unfamiliar words. It shows you how many syllables a word contains and it tells you how to divide the word at the end of a written line. When you divide a word you must always divide it between syllables, never in the middle of a syllable. For example, *doghouse* is divided between *dog-* and *house.* One-syllable words cannot be divided.

The written syllables of a word are divided in the first entry for the word in your dictionary. The entry is in boldface type. Each syllable is shown by a centered dot that separates it from other syllables: **dog·house.**

To determine where to divide a written word into syllables, follow these guidelines:

- Divide words between doubled consonants. A consonant is any letter of the alphabet except the vowels *a, e, i, o, u,* and sometimes *y.* The word *syllable* is a good example. It should be divided as *syl·la·ble.*

- When you have a choice, a new syllable should usually begin with a consonant rather than a vowel. For example, *di·vide,* rather than *div·ide; be·gin,* rather than *beg·in.* Please remember that no rule is absolute, this one included. If you are in doubt about where you should divide a word, check your dictionary.

- When possible, divide words between consonants. Examples: *em·brace, in·struct, ram·ble.* Exception: Do not divide such groupings as *ph, th, ch,* or *sh* as these letters make a single sound.

FINDING GOLD IN THE DICTIONARY
(continued)

PRONUNCIATION

Your dictionary helps you to pronounce its main entry words by showing pronunciation symbols in parentheses, following the entry word. A key to the pronunciation symbols is usually in the front of the dictionary, and part of this key is also printed at the bottom of every page or every other page for easy reference.

Dictionaries may differ in the way they use marking and symbols to indicate pronunciation, but they are also alike in some ways. They have the following in common:

- They all respell words to match the way they sound when spoken.
- Vowels are marked to show you how they should sound.
- Words are divided into syllables to show how they are spoken.
- Accents (the emphasis the voice gives to certain syllables) are marked.

Here is an example—the pronunciation of the word *dictionary* in *Webster's College Dictionary.*

\dĭk'-shə-nĕr'-ē\   Let's start by analyzing the vowels. The first vowel is ĭ. By checking the pronunciation key at the bottom of the right-hand page, you will find that an *i* with this mark over it, ˘ (it looks like a tiny toenail paring), is pronounced like the *i* in *sit*. The next vowel, ə, is a *schwa*, and it sounds like *uh*. An upside-down *e* indicates a schwa sound. The pronunciation key tells us that the next vowel, ĕ, is pronounced like the *e* in *set*. The final vowel, ē has a long mark over it, ¯. It is pronounced like the *e* in *easy*.

Now let's look at the consonants. The *d* is pronounced *d*. The *c* is pronounced *k*. The *ti* is pronounced *sh*. The *n* is pronounced *n*, and the *r* is pronounced *r*.

Now notice the accent marks. The word *dictionary* has two accents, one heavier than the other. The heavy accent, ', shows that the first syllable gets the most emphasis or stress. The light accent, ', shows that the third syllable gets some stress, but not as much as the first.

To become familiar with the pronunciation key in your dictionary, study the explanation at the beginning of the dictionary. As you and your dictionary become better acquainted, you can read the symbols faster and more easily. Eventually, you will not need to use the pronunciation key, except for unusual situations.

Exercise #11 for Practice

Use the following pronunciation key to translate the following quotations into written English. Write your answers in the spaces below. Then check your answers at the end of this section.

\ă\	cat	\ō\	toe
\ā\	pay	\ô\	law, fault
\âr\	pair	\oi\	boil
\ä\	far	\o͝o\	look
\b\	big	\o͞o\	boot, who
\ch\	chip	\ou\	pouch
\d\	day	\p\	pony
\ĕ\	bed	\r\	roam
\ē\	bee	\s\	sink
\f\	faith, phone	\sh\	ship, push
\g\	game	\t\	tip, top
\h\	help	\th\	think
\hw\	what	\t͟h\	that
\ĭ\	spin	\ŭ\	but
\ī\	bite, fry	\ûr\	her, sir, anchor, herd
\îr\	beer, tier	\v\	vault
\j\	jump	\w\	wink
\k\	cat, kite, quite	\y\	yank
\l\	like, funnel	\z\	zebra
\m\	make	\zh\	garage, decision, pleasure
\n\	note, oven	\ə\	seven, bonus, edible
\ng\	sang	\ər\	glitter, urban
\ŏ\	plot		

1. \nĕv'-ər mĭ-stāk' mō'-shən fər ăk'-shən\ —Ernest Hemingway

_____

2. \ī dōnt kâr hwŭt yo͞o ❤ —Bumper sticker

_____

3. \ə stĭch in tīm wo͝od hăv kən-fyo͞ozd' ĭn'-stīn\ —Unknown

_____

4. \hwĕn yo͞o ər āt yĭrz ōld, nŭth'-ing ĭz ĕn'-ē əv yər bĭz'-nəs\ —Lenny Bruce

_____

FINDING GOLD IN THE DICTIONARY (continued)

PARTS OF SPEECH

The dictionary tells us what part of speech a word is. It indicates the part of speech with an abbreviation in italics, placed after the word's pronunciation. Here are the usual abbreviations for the various parts of speech:

n.	= noun	*adj.*	= adjective
pro.	= pronoun	*adv.*	= adverb
v.	= verb	*prep.*	= preposition
v.i.	= verb, intransitive	*conj.*	= conjunction
v.t.	= verb, transitive	*interj.*	= interjection

Many words can be more than one part of speech. For instance, *speed* can be used as a noun: *Our speed increased rapidly*; as a verb: *Don't speed or you will get a ticket*; or as an adjective: *The speed limit is 35 m.p.h.* Different dictionaries handle parts of speech in different ways. Sometimes they provide a separate entry for each part of speech. Sometimes the word has one entry and its various parts of speech and its meanings are all listed after that one entry.

Exercise #12 for Practice

Look up the following words in your dictionary. Indicate what parts of speech each word can be. Write the abbreviations in the spaces provided. Your dictionary may show more than one entry for the word, depending on the system it uses.

Example: *direct*   *v.t., v.i., adj.*

1. front   _____

2. motion   _____

3. promise   _____

4. face   _____

5. horn   _____

HISTORY (ETYMOLOGY)

The etymology or history of a word tells us where and how the word originated and how it developed. Most dictionaries provide this information in a very brief form, either near the beginning or at the end of the entry. The etymology traces a word as far back as possible. It tells you from what language, and in what form, a word came into English; and it even traces the pre-English source as far back as possible.

The English language comes from a language spoken thousands of years ago in north-central Europe called Indo-European. It was a combination of many dialects that had spread over Europe and parts of India.

Different dictionaries may use different abbreviations to indicate a word's origin. In the front of your dictionary you will find a list of abbreviations that tells you what the word origin abbreviations stand for. Here are some examples from *Funk and Wagnall's Standard Dictionary.*

label [<OF, a ribbon, ?< OHG *lappa,* a rag]

> This means that the modern word *label* comes from (<) the Old French word *label*, meaning ''ribbon,'' and that the Old French word perhaps came from the Old High German word *lappa,* meaning ''rag.''

alcohol [Med.L, orig., fine powder <Arabic *al-hoh'l* the powdered antimony]

> The modern word *alcohol* comes from the Medieval Latin word for a ''fine powder,'' derived from the Arabic *al-hoh'l,* ''the powdered antimony'' (a metallic element).

hassle [?, haggle + tussle]

> The question mark means that perhaps—no one is sure—*hassle* is derived from a blending of *haggle* and *tussle.*

FINDING GOLD IN THE DICTIONARY (continued)

Exercise #13 for Practice

Look up the following words in your dictionary and write the etymology for each word in the space provided. Check your answers at the end of the section.

Example: **angel** [ME, fr. OF *angele*, fr. LL *angelus*, fr. Gr. *angelos*, literally messenger]

1. **eye** _____
2. **manual** _____
3. **million** _____
4. **apple** _____
5. **water** _____

SYNONYMS AND ANTONYMS

Synonyms are words that mean nearly the same as the entry word. For example, possible synonyms for the verb *steal* could be *take, rob, snatch, filch, pilfer, embezzle*. Synonyms are usually found at the end of a word entry in your dictionary. Synonyms are especially useful when you wish to emphasize an idea, yet do not want to repeat the same word several times. They are also useful when you want to pinpoint an exact meaning. Sometimes you will find synonyms that express your meaning more exactly than the word you thought of originally.

Exercise #14 for Practice

Find the following words in your dictionary and list one or two synonyms for each one in the space provided. Check possible answers at the end of the section.

Example: **illegal:** unlawful, illicit, criminal

1. **famous** _____
2. **strike** _____
3. **insist** _____
4. **strong** _____
5. **bear** (v.) _____

An antonym is a word that is opposite in meaning from the entry word. *Dark* is the antonym for *light; tall* is the antonym for *short.* Unfortunately, antonyms are not listed in the dictionary as often as synonyms. When they are listed, they appear after the synonyms.

Exercise #15 for Practice

Look up the following words in your dictionary. For each one, list an antonym in the space provided. You may want to use a large, unabridged dictionary, which you will find in a library or a resource center. When you complete the exercise, check your answers at the end of this section.

Example: **big** small (or little, or tiny)

1. **free** _____
2. **happy** _____
3. **polite** _____
4. **good** _____
5. **old** (person) _____

Your dictionary is the most important tool you have to help you build your vocabulary. You can find out how to pronounce words, how to spell them, what they mean, how they function grammatically, what their history (etymology) is, where you divide them at the ends of lines and which words mean the same or the opposite.

Your dictionary has many surprises as well. The larger your dictionary is, the more likely it is to include some or all of the following information: Rules for punctuation and grammar, capitalization rules, a guide for writing footnotes, information on avoiding sexist language, parliamentary procedure, meanings and origins of people's names, famous quotations, U.S. population by cities, definition of abbreviations and the rules for writing research papers. In a sense, your dictionary is like a small encyclopedia. Just for fun, set aside a lunch hour, take a break from television, or walk your dictionary to the park and spend an hour or two becoming acquainted. As you get to know your dictionary you will be rewarded many times over. It is truly one of the most valuable books you own.

A THESAURUS BY ANY OTHER NAME

Another helpful reference book is a thesaurus (pronounced \thə-sôr'-əs\). It is an entire book of synonyms. *Beautiful, attractive, lovely* and *pleasing* are examples of synonyms. The word *thesaurus* comes from the Greek word *thesauros,* meaning "treasure." Writers find a thesaurus especially useful when they are looking for a word to express an exact shade of meaning. For example, *Webster's New World Thesaurus* provides 55 synonyms for *genuine,* including *real, true, actual, proved, tested, good* and so forth.

Although a thesaurus is a useful tool, inexperienced writers sometimes abuse it by looking up big words to make their writing sound important. Like this:

> *Neophytes mistreat synonym lexicons by surveying sesquipedalian terminology to amplify the weightiness of their compositions.*

Many versions of thesauri are available. Here are a few suggestions, but you should explore the options for yourself so that you find one that is right for you. You will find them in the reference section of a library or book store, next to the dictionaries.

► *Roget's International Thesaurus* (Harper and Row) is the oldest and best known. Most purists like this one because it is so complete. However, it is the most difficult to use. The words are grouped in lists of related ideas organized in a specific format. An enormous index at the back of the book tells where a word can be found. Just follow the reference numbers.

► If you are not concerned with such exact shades of meaning, consider the *Doubleday Roget's Thesaurus in Dictionary Form* (Doubleday and Co.). Words are listed from *A* to *Z* with synonyms and antonyms listed under each one. You will find this version easy to use.

► *Webster's New World Thesaurus* (Warner Books) is revised and updated for the 1990s. It is a paperback, with listings in alphabetical order. It includes the latest slang and technical terms, and it is easy to use.

Here are a few things you will *not* find in a thesaurus:

- It is not a dictionary, so it suggests words rather than defining them.
- It is not a grammar book.
- You will not find correct pronunciations, so keep your dictionary handy.
- Spelling and usage are not features (but everything is spelled correctly).

HOW TO USE A THESAURUS

Before using a thesaurus, you should read the directions. As with anything new, you will use it more effectively and enjoy it more if you receive proper instructions. So begin with the introduction or preface at the front of the book. It provides important guidelines and tells you what the book will do for you. Next, read the section entitled "How to Use This Book." Then jump in and explore, search, investigate and examine your thesaurus. Here is a quiz to see how you are progressing. Use a thesaurus that lists its entry words in alphabetical order. (It's easier.) Check your answers at the end of the quiz.

1. In what specific writing situation can a thesaurus be most helpful?

   _____

2. How is a thesaurus different from a dictionary?

   _____

3. List five different types of documents under the category of *record* (noun).

   _____   _____

   _____   _____

   _____

4. Write five synonyms for *rare* (adjective).

   _____   _____

   _____   _____

   _____

5. Find two antonyms for *disturb*.

   _____   _____

6. Find two slang terms for *doctor*.

   _____   _____

ANSWERS TO SECTION 3 EXERCISES

EXERCISE #1

1. yes; **2.** yes; **3.** no; **4.** yes; **5.** yes; **6.** yes; **7.** no; **8.** yes; **9.** no; **10.** yes; **11.** no; **12.** yes

Note: *Tom, Dick, and Harry* is defined in the new *Webster's College Dictionary*. In this day of nonsexist language, perhaps we should change this phrase to *Tom, Dick, and Harriet*.

EXERCISE #2

1. bloomers; **2.** brace; **3.** flake; **4.** grape; **5.** mustard; **6.** sad

EXERCISE #3

1. cape; **2.** cent; **3.** city; **4.** consult; **5.** credit; **6.** cute

EXERCISE #4

1. what; **2.** when; **3.** where; **4.** while; **5.** whom; **6.** why

EXERCISE #5

1. senate; **2.** sensation; **3.** sense; **4.** sensitive; **5.** sensor; **6.** sentence

EXERCISE #6

1. in; **2.** invent; **3.** invert; **4.** invest; **5.** investment; **6.** invoke

EXERCISE #7

1. ant; **2.** anteater; **3.** cut; **4.** cute; **5.** dangle; **6.** jiggle; **7.** jingle; **8.** macaroni; **9.** muscle; **10.** mussel; **11.** must; **12.** shrimp; **13.** shrub; **14.** social; **15.** socialize; **16.** where; **17.** whimper; **18.** wig; **19.** wiggle; **20.** wimp

EXERCISE #8

mainly, maintain, maize, major; lagoon, laid, lake; both, bound, bow

EXERCISE #9

1. *grain:* a small, hard seed, especially the seed of a food plant such as wheat, corn, rye, oats. **2.** *grain:* any small, hard particle such as sand, gold, pepper, or gunpowder. **3.** *grain:* the arrangement or direction of fibers in wood, meat, etc., or the resulting pattern. **4.** *grain:* the smallest possible amount of anything. **5.** *grain:* the smallest unit of weight in the U.S. and British system—equal to 0.002285 ounces. **6.** *pitch:* to throw or toss. **7.** *pitch:* to set or build with a downward slope. **8.** *pitch:* to erect or set up (a tent, a camp, or the like). **9.** *pitch in* (informal): to contribute to a common cause. **10.** *pitch:* to lurch or dive.

EXERCISE #10

1. *ph-;* **2.** *ps* or *c;* **3.** *e;* **4.** *kn* or *gn* or *pn;* **5.** *ps* or *c;* **6.** *ph;* **7.** *g;* **8.** *c;* **9.** *wr;* **10.** *g*

EXERCISE #11

1. Never mistake motion for action. **2.** I don't care what you ♡. **3.** A stitch in time would have confused Einstein. **4.** When you are eight years old, nothing is your business.

EXERCISE #12

1. front: *n., adj., v., interj.;* **2.** motion: *n., v.;* **3.** promise: *n., v.t., v.i.;* **4.** face: *n., v.t., v.i.;* **5.** horn: *n., v., adj.*

EXERCISE #13

1. eye [bef. 900; ME *eie, ie,* OE *ege,* var. of *eage;* c. OS *oga,* OHG *ouga,* ON *auga* Go *augo;* akin to L *oculus,* Gk *ops,* Skt, *aski*]; **2. manual** [1400–50; late ME (<MF) < L *manualis* (adj.), *manuale* (n.) (something that can be held in the hand = *manu(s)* hand + *alis, ale*] **3. million** [1350–1400; ME *millione* = *mille* thousand (<L) + *-one* aug. suffix] **4. apple** [bef. 900; ME; OE *aeppel,* C. OFris *appel,* OS *apl, appul,* OHG *apful,* Crimean Go *apel*] **5. water** [bef. 900; ME; OE *waeter,* c. OS *watar,* OHG *wazzar;* akin to ON *vain,* Go *wato,* Hittite *watter,* Gk *hydor*]

ANSWERS TO SECTION 3 EXERCISES
(continued)

EXERCISE #14

1. famous: eminent, illustrious, foremost, noted, celebrated;   **2. strike:** beat, hit, punch;   **3. insist:** persevere, persist, repeat;   **4. strong:** hardy, robust, sinewy, stalwart;   **5. bear** (*v.*): abide, carry, endure, support

EXERCISE #15

1. free: bound, dependent, enslaved;   **2. happy:** unhappy, distressed, gloomy, pensive;   **3. polite:** rude, uncivil, impolite;   **4. good:** bad, unjust, unworthy, negative;   **5. old:** young, youthful, junior

ANSWERS TO THESAURUS QUIZ

1. Finding synonyms and subtle word differences.   **2.** Words in a thesaurus are not defined.   **3.** memo, catalog, list, schedule, contract;   **4.** sparse, few, meager, limited, precious;   **5.** quiet, calm;   **6.** sawbones, doc

S E C T I O N

4

Uprooting Root Words

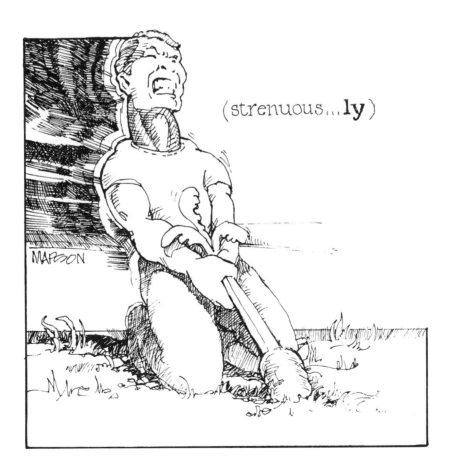

(strenuous...ly)

MAKING VOCABULARY STUDY EASY

With so many words in the English language, we need an easy method for taming the task of learning new vocabulary. Fortunately, word-lovers before us have eased the way. Through their studies they discovered that words break naturally into separate elements. Like a good story, words have a beginning, a middle, and an end. We have learned from lexicographers (people who study words) to create and change words by simply adding or subtracting a few letters from the basic word element called a **root word.** For example, the root word *wise* becomes *unwise* by adding *un-* to the beginning of the word. It changes again by adding *-ly* to the end of the word: *unwisely.* When we add letters to the front of a root word to change its meaning, we are adding a **prefix.** When letters are added to the end of a root word to change its meaning, we are adding a **suffix.**

In the word *unwise, un-* is a prefix meaning "not." The prefix changes the meaning of the word *wise* to "not wise." The suffix *-ly* means "like" or "in that manner." So, *unwisely* means "not in a wise manner." Prefixes, suffixes, and roots are valuable because they keep their same meanings even when used with different words. Therefore, *un-* means "not," when used with other root words as well: *unhappy, unskilled, untried, unstable.*

By learning some of the common prefixes, suffixes and roots you can increase your vocabulary by several thousand words without much difficulty. Suddenly you will command a Niagara of words simply by using various prefixes, suffixes and root words. This knowledge makes vocabulary study much easier and a lot more fun. Be warned, however, that rules for joining these word units can be a bit slippery. Prefixes may change form, and sometimes letters are doubled to ease pronunciation. But when you learn the basics, you will not quibble over a few exceptions.

MAKING VOCABULARY STUDY EASY
(continued)

ROOT WORDS

A root word is the original word, or the word within a word that carries the main meaning. Other word parts are added to modify or change the root meaning. For example, the word *transmitting* consists of *trans-mitt-ing.* (The *t* is doubled for spelling purposes.) The root word is *mit*, meaning ''to send.'' This root word can be combined with prefixes and suffixes to form new words—for example: *remitting, omitting, committing* and *admitting.* Root words are often from Latin or Greek.

PREFIXES

A prefix is an addition of one or more letters at the beginning of a root word to alter or modify its meaning. Like roots, prefixes are not words in themselves. In the following examples the root *spire,* ''to breathe,'' is changed by different prefixes:

inspire
perspire
conspire
expire
transpire

SUFFIXES

A suffix is a letter or group of letters added to the end of a root word. Suffixes change the meaning of the root word somewhat and identify its part of speech (verb, noun, adjective, adverb, etc.). For example, by adding different suffixes, the verb *prospect* changes to *prospector* (noun) or *prospective* (adjective).

A word of caution: The meaning of a word is not always an exact translation of its prefix, root and suffix. *Paradox*, if translated literally, means ''beyond + opinion.'' However, the dictionary definition is ''a contradiction that may be true.'' Also, *impasse* does not mean ''not to pass.'' It is defined as ''a dilemma or a dead end.'' Use prefixes, suffixes and roots to get you into the territory of the correct meaning, then use the context of the sentence for more information. The context is the other words in the sentence that influence the unknown word you wish to define.

COMMON LATIN ROOTS

Think of root words as the building blocks of your vocabulary. They form the core of your word, then the prefix and suffix cluster around it. Latin and Greek roots are the foundations of 60–70 percent of our words. Following are twenty Latin roots and fifteen Greek roots. They are only a few of many roots (our language is well-rooted), but they are some of the most common. At first they may all look like "Greek" to you. Do not be discouraged. Read through the list and find those you recognize. Then choose those you want to learn and make 3×5 cards listing the root word, its Latin or Greek meaning, and examples.

	Root	Meaning	Examples
1.	cede, ceed, cess	go, move, yield	recede, exceed, access, proceed, recess
2.	cred	believe	credible, credit, credential
3.	dict	speak, say	dictionary, predict, dictate
4.	duce, duct	lead, take, bring	seduce, conduct, abduct, production
5.	fac, fig, fic	do, make	factory, figure, fiction
6.	fer	carry, bring	offer, transfer, refer, fertile
7.	gress, grad	step, go	progress, congress, graduate, degrade
8.	ject	throw, cast	reject, project, adjective, abject
9.	mit, miss	send	transmit, permission, missile
10.	port	carry	report, export, portable
11.	scrib, script	write	describe, subscription, scribble
12.	spec, spect	look	speculate, inspect, spectacle
13.	struct	build	structure, instruct, obstruct
14.	tend, tens	stretch, strain	tendon, extend, tension
15.	test	witness	testimony, testify, protest
16.	tract	pull, draw	tractor, retract, distract
17.	ven, vent	come, move forward	avenue, event, convent, adventure
18.	verse, vert	turn	reverse, advertise, pervert
19.	vid, vide, vis,	see, look	video, provide, invisible
20.	voc, voke	call	vocation, vocabulary, revoke

COMMON LATIN ROOTS (continued)

Exercise #1 for Practice

Extending Your Latin Roots

Here is a brief exercise to help you recognize Latin roots easily. Find and underline the root in each of the following words. Check your answers at the end of the section.

1. adverse
2. incredible
3. injection
4. avid
5. ferment

6. object
7. important
8. invention
9. contradict
10. reduction

Greek Roots

Root	Meaning	Examples
1. *arch*	rule	monarch, archive, anarchy
2. *auto*	self	automatic, autograph
3. *bio*	life	biology, bionic
4. *chron*	time	chronic, chronicle
5. *geo*	earth	geography, geology
6. *gen*	birth	generate, genius, Genesis
7. *hydr*	water	dehydrate, hydrant, hydrogen
8. *log, ology*	thought, science	logic, logo, astrology
9. *meter*	measure	thermometer, diameter, perimeter
10. *pan*	all	panorama, pancreas, pantomime
11. *path*	feeling	apathy, sympathy, pathology
12. *phil*	friend, lover	Philadelphia, philander, philosophy
13. *phob*	fear	acrophobia, agoraphobia
14. *phon*	sound	telephone, symphony, phonograph
15. *soph*	wisdom	sophomore, sophisticated

Exercise #2 for Practice

Extending Your Greek Roots

Underline the Greek root words to help you recognize them more easily. Check your answers at the end of the section.

1. barometer
2. pathetic
3. panacea
4. microphone
5. automobile

6. hydraulic
7. philatelist
8. generous
9. biopsy
10. synchronicity

Exercise #3 for Practice

Digging Deeper

Match the Greek and Latin roots in the first column with their meanings in the second column. Place the correct letter of the meaning on the line next to the root that it matches. Check your answers at the end of the section.

1. _____ *fer*
2. _____ *voc*
3. _____ *chron*
4. _____ *pan*
5. _____ *phon*
6. _____ *dict*
7. _____ *port*
8. _____ *cred*
9. _____ *soph*
10. _____ *phob*
11. _____ *gress*
12. _____ *spect*
13. _____ *tract*
14. _____ *arch*
15. _____ *phil*

a. pull
b. fear
c. call
d. speak
e. step
f. believe
g. time
h. look
i. sound
j. rule
k. carry
l. friend
m. all
n. wisdom
o. carry

COMMON PREFIXES

Many prefixes keep their original spellings when attached to root words, but others do not. For easier pronunciation, the spelling of a prefix sometimes changes when it is added to a root: *ex-* + *mit* = *emit*; *sub-* + *fer* = *suffer*; *com-* + *equal* = *coequal*. Some prefixes look alike when they are attached to roots; for example, *hyper-* and *hypo-*, *ante-* and *anti-*. Be careful because these prefixes do not mean the same thing.

Prefix	Meaning	Examples
1. *ab-*	away from, against	abject, abolish, absent
2. *ad-*	to, toward	admit, admire, adhere
3. *anti-*	against	antibiotic, anticlimax, antidote
4. *com-, con-*	together, with	compress, connect, contain
5. *de-*	away, down	devalue, decide, defer
6. *dis-*	apart, out	dismiss, disarm, disable
7. *ex-*	out	express, exit, expect
8. *homo-*	same	Homo sapiens, homogenized
9. *in-, i-*	not	indefinite, irresponsible, illegal
10. *inter-*	between	intermediate, interim
11. *mal-*	bad, evil	malpractice, maladjusted, malice
12. *mis-*	wrong	mistake, misplace, mislead, misspell
13. *per-*	through	persuade, persecute
14. *post-*	after	postpone, posthaste
15. *pre-*	before	preview, predict, prevent
16. *pro-*	for, in place of	pronoun, project, provide
17. *re-*	back, again	report, react, respond
18. *sub-*	under	submarine, submit, subside
19. *trans-*	across	transport, transcend, transcribe
20. *un-*	not	uneasy, uncommon, unthinkable

Exercise #4 for Practice

Using Negative Prefixes

In the sentences below, write the correct word in each blank space.
Check your answers at the end of the section.

      Example: To distort something is to bend it __out__ of shape.

1. On "Star Trek," when Mr. Spock says something is illogical, he means
   that it does _____ make sense.

2. Something that is illicit is _____ legal.

3. To disconnect an electrical cord is to pull it _____ of the socket.

4. An inflexible person is one who is _____ flexible.

5. If you are _____ happy, you are unhappy.

6. Someone who is antisocial does _____ go to parties.

Exercise #5 for Practice

Positives to Negatives

Give the negative forms of the following words. Check your answers at
the end of the section.

1. likely _____

2. active _____

3. honor _____

4. regular _____

5. legible _____

COMMON PREFIXES (continued)

Exercise #6 for Practice

Which Prefix Is Correct?

Check the correct prefix (a or b) in the following exercise. Check your answers at the end of the section.

1. a. compact _____   b. conpact _____
2. a. disbehave _____   b. misbehave _____
3. a. provide _____   b. pervide _____
4. a. interim _____   b. innerim _____
5. a. adbolish _____   b. abolish _____

Exercise #7 for Practice

Refix the Prefix

In each of the sentences below, choose the correct word from the list and write it in the blank space. Check your answers at the end of the section.

Example: People who think that a war is wrong may __*protest*__ against it.

submarine	misplaced	disagree	transmit
postponed	homogenized	repeat	protest
concert	abject	international	

1. If you do not agree with your manager, you should agree to
   _____.
2. When someone does not hear you the first time, you must
   _____ what you said.
3. Milk is _____ when the cream and skim are mixed together.
4. Trade between two nations is called _____ trade.
5. A report that is lost because it is put on the wrong desk is
   _____.
6. A ship that travels under water is a _____.
7. When a group of musicians play to an audience, they are giving a
   _____.
8. To send a fax over the phone line is to _____ the message.
9. Someone who is thrown into a penniless state is living in
   _____ poverty.
10. A project that is put off until later is _____.

SUFFIXES

Suffixes come at the end of a word. They are not as important as prefixes and roots, but they serve as tags to change words from one part of speech to another. You will benefit from studying suffixes because they help to resolve annoying spelling problems. And they are a good review of grammar terms and uses. Suffixes provide flexibility because you can use them to change a word from a noun to a verb, or vice versa, as in *apology* (noun) to *apologize* (verb), or *depend* (verb) to *dependent* (noun).

When you change a word from one part of speech to another, endings will not always be neat and clear. The same suffix may have different spellings: descend*ent* and reli*ant*. Do not let such foibles bother you. Let the word-gurus worry about them. Instead, spend your time learning the suffixes that you need in order to improve your vocabulary skills. Start with the most interesting word endings and enjoy the process.

Noun Suffixes

To refresh our memories: a noun is a word used to name a person (the president), place (a city), thing (an apple), animal (a unicorn), group (the navy), or idea (democracy). The following suffixes identify a word as being a noun.

Noun Suffix	Meaning	Examples
1. *-ence, -ance, -ency*	condition of	presence, attendance, presidency
2. *-dom*	state or condition of	kingdom, wisdom
3. *-er, -or, -ress*	one who does the activity	painter, doctor, actress
4. *-ism*	doctrine, act	materialism, mannerism
5. *-ist*	one who supports a doctrine	feminist, socialist
6. *-hood*	state of	childhood, statehood, manhood
7. *-ment*	state, quality, act	statement, testament
8. *-ness*	state of	shyness, fondness, kindness
9. *-tion*	performance of an act or activity	transaction, graduation, function
10. *-ity*	state of	reality, humanity

SUFFIXES (continued)

Exercise #8 for Practice

Words into Nouns

Can you delete letters when necessary and then add suffixes to make these root words into nouns? Write in the correct noun for each word and check your answers at the end of the section.

1. disrupt _____   4. gentle _____

2. free _____   5. rely _____

3. excite _____

Adjective Suffixes

An adjective is a word that modifies or describes a noun or a pronoun. You can recognize adjectives by their endings and by their placement in the sentence (in front of nouns and pronouns). Some common adjective suffixes are listed below.

Adjective Suffix	Meaning	Examples
1. -*able*, -*ible*	able to, capable of	visible, portable, curable
2. -*ful*	full of	careful, awful, joyful
3. -*ish*	like, related to	childish
4. -*ive*	having the power of	disruptive, explosive, productive
5. -*less*	without	hopeless, useless
6. -*ic*, -*ac*	like, related to	angelic, cardiac
7. -*ory*, -*ary*	relating to, like	sensory, military, stationary
8. -*ous*, -*ose*	full of, like	perilous, enormous, verbose
9. -*ward*	in the direction of	eastward, homeward, outward
10. -*y*	possessing	gloomy, sunny, thirsty

Exercise #9 for Practice

Words into Adjectives

Convert each of the following five nouns into adjectives. Change endings where necessary. Check your answers at the end of the section.

1. thought _____   4. west _____
2. danger _____   5. smell _____
3. time _____

Verb Suffixes

Verbs express action or existence. They are defined by their endings, and by the role they play in a sentence. Here are some verb suffixes. There are not as many verb suffixes as noun or adjective suffixes.

Verb Suffix	Meaning	Examples
1. *-ate*	act in that way	appreciate, facilitate
2. *-en*	cause to become	weaken, sharpen, redden
3. *-ify*	make into, form	qualify, verify, signify
4. *-ize*	cause to become	symbolize, itemize, criticize

Exercise #10 for Practice

Words into Verbs

Can you add a suffix and turn these words into verbs? You will have to change the spelling in two of the words in order to add a suffix. Write your answers in the blank spaces below. Check your answers at the end of the section.

1. origin _____
2. fantasy _____
3. wide _____
4. loose _____
5. electric _____

ANSWERS TO SECTION 4 EXERCISES

EXERCISE #1

1. ad*verse*;   2. in*cred*ible;   3. in*ject*ion;   4. a*vid*;   5. *ferment*;   6. ob*ject*;
7. im*port*ant;   8. in*vent*ion;   9. contra*dict*;   10. re*duct*ion

EXERCISE #2

1. baro*meter*;   2. *path*etic;   3. *pan*acea;   4. micro*phone*;   5. *auto*mobile;
6. *hydr*aulic;   7. *phil*atelist;   8. *gen*erous;   9. *bio*psy;   10. syn*chron*icity

EXERCISE #3

1. k;   2. c;   3. g;   4. m;   5. i;   6. d;   7. k;   8. f;   9. n;   10. b;   11. e;   12. h;
13. a;   14. j;   15. l

EXERCISE #4

1. not;   2. not;   3. out;   4. not;   5. not;   6. not

EXERCISE #5

1. unlikely;   2. inactive;   3. dishonor;   4. irregular;   5. illegible

EXERCISE #6

1. a;   2. b;   3. a;   4. a;   5. b

EXERCISE #7

1. disagree;   2. repeat;   3. homogenized;   4. international;   5. misplaced;
6. submarine;   7. concert;   8. transmit;   9. abject;   10. postponed

EXERCISE #8

1. disruption;   2. freedom;   3. excitement;   4. gentleness;   5. reliance

EXERCISE #9

1. thoughtful (or thoughtless);   2. dangerous;   3. timely (or timeless);
4. westward;   5. smelly

EXERCISE #10

1. originate;   2. fantasize;   3. widen;   4. loosen;   5. electrify

SECTION

5

Building a
Strong Vocabulary

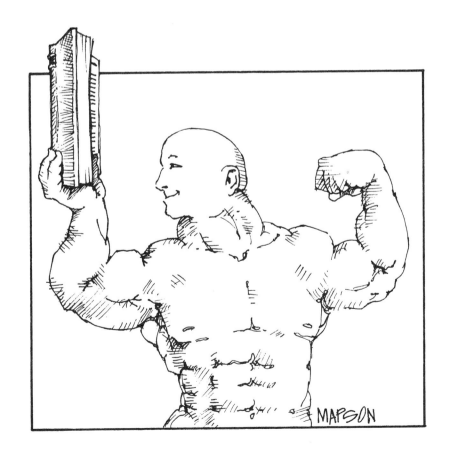

50 WORDS MADE EASY

This chapter highlights fifty important words that you should recognize when you see them or hear them. Study these words carefully and work through the exercises. Soon you will be using all fifty words easily. These words appear often in business communications, in newspapers, on television and in movies. However, we chose them because they often appear in spelling and vocabulary lists for the GED (high school equivalency exam) and other standardized tests for vocabulary knowledge and job placement.

Fifty words is an important beginning. From these exercises you will learn how to build your word power, then you can apply these skills to other words you wish to master. We have divided the fifty words into five sections of ten words each. Each new word is presented in a form used by most dictionaries.

First you will find the alphabetized entry word, its pronunciation, the part of speech, and a simple etymology (history). Next you will find the definition(s) of the word, along with sentences in which each definition is used correctly. Finally, synonyms and antonyms are listed, where relevant. Following each section you will find a set of exercises to help you practice your new words.

To speed your improvement, work through the first section, then use as many of the new words as you can at work or at school for the next few days. Write the more difficult words on a piece of paper with their definitions, put them in your purse or pocket, and glance at them from time to time. Read the newspaper or a magazine and use a yellow highlighter pen to mark these new words as you find them. It is important to use your new vocabulary at every opportunity. When you have mastered the words in the first section, go on to the second section. Be playful. Buy a box of small silver stars and place them next to the words you already know, or have recently learned. (Of course you will not want to do this on your business letters and memos.)

WORD LIST PRE-QUIZ

The following vocabulary quiz contains the fifty words in this section. Circle the letter that provides the closest definition to the vocabulary word in bold type. Check your answers at the end of the quiz. When you complete the quiz you will know which words to work on, so begin with the first word you missed and go from there. Put stars next to those you answered correctly. Soon you will have enough stars to start your own galaxy.

1. **abject**   (a) agreeable (b) hateful (c) miserable (d) wealthy

2. **adverse**   (a) unfavorable (b) opposite (c) poetic (d) supportive

3. **aggregate**   (a) clumsy (b) nerdy (c) informed (d) collective

4. **allege**   (a) a rim (b) claim (c) disown (d) simplify

5. **allude**   (a) refer (b) climb (c) indecent (d) repeat

6. **askew**   (a) questioning (b) crooked (c) sticky (d) backward

7. **astute**   (a) helpful (b) aware (c) useless (d) rubberized

8. **augment**   (a) fight (b) increase (c) explain (d) pout

9. **avid**   (a) greedy (b) birdlike (c) eager (d) useful

10. **benign**   (a) good (b) interesting (c) thankful (d) different

11. **boycott**   (a) a bed for a male child (b) exclude (c) support (d) escape

12. **cajole**   (a) hunt (b) sacrifice (c) coax (d) scare

13. **candid**   (a) photogenic (b) easily led (c) narrow (d) straightforward

14. **chronic**   (a) laid back (b) useful (c) recurring (d) old

15. **cogent**   (a) convincing (b) warm (c) lively (d) thankful

16. **condone**   (a) consume (b) approve (c) thank (d) avoid

17. **copious**   (a) written (b) abundant (c) boring (d) helpful

18. **deviate**   (a) spin (b) mumble (c) move (d) digress

19. **diligent** (a) smart (b) persistent (c) undecided (d) scared witless

20. **discourse** (a) direction (b) opposite of "dat course" (c) sentiment
    (d) conversation

21. **docile** (a) unwilling (b) pleasing (c) manageable (d) correct

22. **eminent** (a) high ranking (b) emerging (c) well made (d) state

23. **ethical** (a) gas guzzling (b) immoral (c) honest (d) devout

24. **exploit** (a) look around (b) renounce (c) take advantage of (d) unemployed

25. **flaunt** (a) dabble (b) display boldly (c) fold (d) blunt

26. **foible** (a) metal screw (b) social grace (c) a curse (d) personality quirk

27. **gullible** (a) easily deceived (b) likes sea birds (c) shy (d) well organized

28. **heinous** (a) rebellious (b) evil (c) timely (d) sensitive

29. **impasse** (a) failure (b) deadlock (c) threat (d) heart transplant

30. **inherent** (a) sudden wealth (b) to breathe in (c) innate (d) bird like

31. **irony** (a) housework (b) metalwork (c) childish fear (d) double meaning

32. **lucid** (a) plastic covering (b) clear (c) insane (d) vulgar

33. **novice** (a) beginner (b) author (c) winner (d) religious

34. **paradox** (a) two doctors (b) boat landings (c) contradiction (d) killer bee

35. **perjure** (a) swear falsely (b) buy on credit (c) crush (d) join

36. **premise** (a) oath (b) rule (c) basis for belief (d) treatment of a problem

37. **prolific** (a) receptive (b) productive (c) famous (d) painful

38. **quell** (a) taste (b) suppress (c) fight (d) flock of birds

39. **raze** (a) lift (b) tear down (c) sharpen (d) act hastily

WORD LIST PRE-QUIZ (continued)

40. **rescind** (a) rewrite (b) reorder (c) renew (d) revoke

41. **ruse** (a) trick (b) use again (c) plan (d) regret

42. **salient** (a) salty (b) valuable (c) prominent (d) sickly

43. **schism** (a) modern dance (b) division (c) union (d) opinion

44. **secular** (a) worldly (b) divided (c) religious (d) outrageous

45. **strident** (a) harsh (b) tooth decay (c) soft (d) stubborn

46. **tacit** (a) dangle (b) specific (c) unspoken (d) angle

47. **thwart** (a) promote (b) destroy (c) scare (d) block

48. **usurp** (a) serve breakfast (b) chase frogs (c) seize power (d) sympathize

49. **vie** (a) compete (b) complete (c) gripe (d) shun

50. **zenith** (a) television (b) a smug look (c) useful information (d) highest point

Answers: 1 c, 2 a, 3 d, 4 b, 5 a, 6 b, 7 b, 8 b, 9 c, 10 a, 11 b, 12 c, 13 d, 14 c, 15 a, 16 b, 17 b, 18 d, 19 d, 20 d, 21 c, 22 a, 23 a, 24 c, 25 b, 26 d, 27 a, 28 b, 29 b, 30 c, 31 d, 32 b, 33 a, 34 c, 35 a, 36 c, 37 b, 38 b, 39 b, 40 d, 41 a, 42 c, 43 b, 44 a, 45 a, 46 c, 47 d, 48 c, 49 a, 50 d

FIRST GROUP: 1. abject – 10. benign

1. abject (AB jekt) *adjective*

[Latin *abjectus*, from *abjicere*, to throw away; from *ab*, away, + *jacere*, to throw]

Definition   a. Utterly miserable, wretched, or cast down.

   Thomas made an **abject** apology because he was ashamed of acting so badly.

   b. Mean, worthless, low-down, or contemptible.

   Only an **abject** coward would turn his back on a helpless victim in distress.

   c. Complete, submissive, unrelieved, or servile.

   June ran from the room screaming in **abject** terror at the sight of a large spider.

Synonyms: pitiful, base, meek, scummy, squalid

2. adverse (ad VURS, AD vurs) *adjective*

[Latin *ad*, against, + *vertere*, to turn]

Definition   Opposing, unfavorable, or antagonistic.

   Although the team received **adverse** criticism from the newspapers, they were supported by their faithful fans.

Note: Do not confuse **adverse** with the related adjective *averse*, meaning ''strongly opposed'' or ''displeased.'' *Adverse* (with a *d*) is used to indicate that plans have gone contrary to a person's wishes. *Averse* (without the *d*) means that the person himself is opposed or reluctant. *Averse* is usually followed by the word *to*. Note the following sentences.

Upper management noted an **adverse** reaction by the employees to the new quality program.

The employees were **averse** to the changes that the quality program would require.

Synonyms: negative, contrary, opposite, unfortunate, unfriendly

Antonyms: favorable, friendly, propitious

FIRST GROUP: 1. abject – 10. benign (continued)

3. **aggregate** (AG ruh git, AG ruh GATE) *noun and adjective*
(AG ruh gate) *verb*

[Latin *ad*, to, + *grex, gregis*, flock, = *aggregare*, to join together]

Definition   (noun) A mass or sum total of individual parts.

> A new house is an **aggregate** of stone, brick and lumber.

(adjective) Total; united; combined; collective.

> The **aggregate** result of combining work space was overcrowding.

(verb) To bring together or bring into a total mass or sum.

> The finance committee **aggregated** funds from several accounts to raise money for the Olympic hopefuls.

Synonyms   (nouns): assemblage, amalgamation, conglomeration, cluster; (adjectives): net, composite; (verbs): accumulate, pile, heap up, consolidate, amalgamate, collect

4. **allege** (uh LEJ) *verb*

[Old English *alegen*, to bring forward as evidence; Latin *ex*, out, + *litigare*, to dispute at law]

Definition   To declare or assert without proof that something is true or correct.

> The mansion on Highbrow Boulevard is **alleged** to be worth $10 million.

> Florence **alleged** that she had seen extraterrestrial beings while hiking near Sedona.

Note: The use of the word **allege** often implies that some doubt exists about the truth of a statement, as in the second example above. At other times, the word **alleged** is used as an adjective and implies that a person wishes to disclaim responsibility for the truth of whatever follows—"the **alleged** expert" or "an **alleged** miracle drug."

Synonyms: claim, declare, assert, affirm, avow

5. allude (uh LOOD) *verb*

[Latin *alludere,* to refer to playfully; from *ad,* to + *ludere,* to play]

Definition   To refer to indirectly or casually.

> During the interview, Shanna **alluded** to her experiences as a member of a self-managing team.

Note: Be careful not to confuse the following words:

1. **allude** (to refer to indirectly) and *elude* (evade, escape, or avoid)
2. **allusive** (suggestive) and *elusive* (hard to grasp or difficult to find)
3. **allusion** (an indirect reference) and *illusion* (a false belief or perception)

Synonyms: hint, refer, suggest, intimate, insinuate

6. askew (uh SKYOO) *adjective and adverb*

[Derivation uncertain but probably Middle English *askue, ascue*]

Definition   a. (adjective and adverb) To one side; crooked; awry; out of line.

> Every piece of furniture in the office was knocked **askew** by the earthquake.

   b. (adverb) Disapprovingly; scornfully.

> Thelma glanced **askew** at Raoul's awful table manners.

Note: There is a subtle difference between the words **askew** and *awry.* **Askew** usually refers to concrete objects like street signs and hats. *Awry,* on the other hand, is generally used for more abstract things like activities, plans and procedures.

Synonyms   (adjectives): lopsided, cock-eyed, uneven; (adverbs): disdainfully, derisively, askance

Antonyms   (adjectives): straight, symmetrical; (adverbs): benignly, approvingly

FIRST GROUP: 1. abject – 10. benign (continued)

7. astute (uh STOOT) *adjective*

[Latin *astutus*, cunning; from *astus*, guile]

Definition   Keenly aware; perceptive; discerning; clever or shrewd, especially in practical matters.

Be an **astute** observer of life first; you can distort it later [paraphrased from Mark Twain].

Our company earned money in the fourth quarter by **astute** speculation in the stock market.

Synonyms: sharp, acute, sagacious, judicious, far-sighted, quick-witted, clever, perceptive

Antonyms: obtuse, undiscerning, stupid, foolish, inane

8. augment (awg MENT) *verb*

[Latin *augmentum*, an increase]

Definition   To enlarge in size, number or strength; to increase.

The general **augmented** the troops with front-line reinforcements.

Twyla planned to **augment** her income with a second job to pay for her new car.

Synonyms: expand, extend, magnify, reinforce, strengthen, fortify

Antonyms: decrease, reduce, curtail, diminish, contract, shrink, shrivel, abate, slacken, dwindle

9. avid (AV ud) *adjective*

[Latin *avidus*; from *avidere*, to crave]

Definition   Extremely eager, keen, ardent, or greedy.

My father has always been an **avid** fisherman.

Avid football fans threw tomatoes at the unpopular referee.

Synonyms: zealous, fervent, gung ho, rabid, fanatical

Antonyms: indifferent, apathetic, unresponsive

10. benign (bi NYNE) *adjective*

[Latin *bene*, well, + *genus*, birth = *benignus*, kind]

Definition Kind and gracious; gentle, good.

The neighbor's dog had a **benign** face and a nasty temper.

A **benign** tumor is not malignant.

Synonyms: benevolent, favorable, helpful, loving

Antonyms: mean, wicked, bad, evil, malevolent, pernicious, injurious

Now that you have reviewed the first ten words, take a few minutes to build your vocabulary muscles by completing the following exercises. They will help you retain what you have learned. Work carefully with the intention of strengthening your recognition and your ability to use each word correctly. You can easily incorporate these words into your vocabulary by giving these exercises a thorough workout. Then keep your word skills in top condition through regular mental exercise.

Exercise #1 for Practice

Quick Check

Match each word in the first column with its definition in the second column. Check your answers at the end of the section.

1. _____ abject	a. refer
2. _____ adverse	b. unfavorable
3. _____ aggregate	c. claim
4. _____ allege	d. aware
5. _____ allude	e. enlarge
6. _____ askew	f. eager
7. _____ astute	g. miserable
8. _____ augment	h. good
9. _____ avid	i. collective
10. _____ benign	j. crooked

FIRST GROUP: 1. abject – 10. benign (continued)

Exercise #2 for Practice

Complete the Sentence

In the ten sentences that follow, fill the blanks with the correct word from the list below. Remember, you don't need a big vocabulary full of polysyllabic (four or more syllables) zingers. You need a confident vocabulary that will help you express yourself with ease. Mastering these ten words is a positive step toward building your confidence and skill.

abject   allude   avid
adverse   askew   benign
aggregate   astute   allege
augment

1. Little Sally appeared in the doorway with her hat _____, her shoes on the wrong feet and her dress on backward.

2. A casserole is an _____ of meat, vegetables and sauce.

3. Fritz is an _____ observer of business trends in Europe and Japan.

4. Mordecai's _____ poverty left him without hope for himself or his family.

5. Vitashot Corporation hopes to _____ its insurance program to include dental coverage for all employees.

6. Theophilus prefers not to fly in small planes in _____ weather.

7. Ryan is such an _____ reader that he checks out three books a week from the library.

8. Bethany may _____ that Roscoe cheated on his exam, but she cannot prove it.

9. When you _____ to my musical ability, please wipe the smile from your face.

10. Alexander has a _____ smile and a pleasing personality to match.

Exercise #3 for Practice

Odds Out

Each number below is followed by four words. Three of them are related in meaning. Cross out the word that does not fit with the others. Check your answers at the end of the section.

1. abject   worthless   miserable   dishonest

2. unfavorable   opposite   adverse   useful

3. cluster   trend   aggregate   sum total

4. forfeit   imply   allege   suggest

5. allude   avoid   refer   hint

6. crooked   awry   awesome   askew

7. acute   astute   perceptive   stoic

8. augment   increase   enlarge   endorse

9. inept   eager   greedy   avid

10. good   benign   robust   kind

SECOND GROUP:
11. boycott – 20. discourse

11. **boycott** (BOI kot) *noun and verb*

[After Charles C. Boycott, a land agent in County Mayo, Ireland, who was put under a ban by his neighbors during the Land League agitation in Ireland in 1880 for refusing to lower rents on the lands he managed.]

Definition   (verb) Joining together to refuse to buy (or) use something or deal with someone as a form of protest.

Protestors plan to **boycott** foreign products to voice their disapproval of unfair trade laws.

(noun) The instance of such practice.

During the civil rights movement of the 1950s and 1960s, both blacks and whites used **boycotts** to protest the evils of segregation.

Synonyms   (verbs): ban, ostracize, blacklist, exclude, object, protest; (nouns): ban, embargo, strike

Antonyms   (verbs): patronize, fraternize with, support, sanction, endorse, approve

12. **cajole** (kuh JOHL) *verb*

[French *cajoler*, to coax]

Definition   To persuade by flattery or false promises.

Suzanna was good at flattery, but even she could not **cajole** Bart into taking her to a movie.

Even though the cause was worthy, Erika could not **cajole** Scrooge into contributing a single dime.

Synonyms: coax, lure, wheedle, inveigle, beguile, induce

Antonyms: dissuade, deter, discourage, turn down

13. candid (KAN ded) *adjective*

[Latin *candidus*, white, pure; from *candere*, to be white or hot]

Definition   a. Frank, outspoken, open and sincere.

> Virilena's **candid** manner charmed her European visitors who enjoyed her forthright descriptions of American customs.

b. Free from bias; straightforward; impartial.

> The alert bystander gave the police a **candid** account of the train accident.

c. Informal; unposed.

> The **candid** photos taken at the Christmas office party showed that "a good time was had by all."

Synonyms: balanced, freely spoken, telling it like it is, genuine, forthright

Antonyms: partial, biased, prejudiced, reserved, evasive, affected

14. chronic (KRON ik) *adjective*

[Greek *chronikos*, of or for the time; from *chronos*, time]

Definition   Continuing for a long time or recurring often; constant.

> Cheryl's inability to be anywhere on time has become a **chronic** problem.

> The Middle East seems to be in a **chronic** state of war.

Note: When used as a medical term, **chronic** describes an ailment that develops slowly and only gradually becomes serious or fatal—for example, arthritis or heart disease. The opposite is *acute*, a medical problem that comes on suddenly and takes only a short time to become serious—for example, a gall bladder attack.

Synonyms: enduring, long-lasting, deep-rooted, ingrained, recurrent

Antonyms: temporary, occasional, incidental, infrequent

SECOND GROUP: 11. boycott – 20. discourse (continued)

15. cogent (KOH junt) *adjective*

[Latin *cogens, cogentis,* driving together; from *co,* a form of *cum,* together + *agere,* to drive]

Definition   Powerfully convincing and believable; to the point.

Yesterday's newspaper contained a **cogent** argument for nationalizing health insurance.

Gwendolyn provided a **cogent** description of the reorganization plan.

Synonyms: powerful, potent, skillful, valid, telling, persuasive, apropos

Antonyms: weak, ineffective, inane, invalid, irrelevant

16. condone (kun DOHN) *verb*

[Latin *condonare,* to give up; from *con,* a form of *cum,* completely + *donare,* to give]

Definition   To overlook; to permit to happen; to pardon an offense, thereby implying forgiveness or possibly approval.

The manager seemed to **condone** Frederick's continual lateness, as he simply ignored it.

Beatrix felt she could no longer **condone** her husband's drinking.

Synonyms: ignore, accept, stomach, put up with, tolerate, be broadminded about

Antonyms: condemn, disapprove, decry, revile, protest, denounce

17. copious (KOH pee us) *adjective*

[Latin *copiosus,* plentiful, from *copia,* abundance]

Definition   Large in number; full; abundant; plentiful.

Geraldo took **copious** notes during the board meeting.

Granny gives **copious** advice about everything from canning plums to raising teenagers.

Synonyms: ample, bountiful, profuse, numerous, lavish

Antonyms: meager, barren, scanty, scarce, sparse

18. deviate (DEE vee ate) *verb*; (DEE vee it) *noun*

[Latin *deviatus*, from *deviare*, to turn aside from; from *de*, away from + *via*, road]

Definition   (verb) To move away from; to turn aside, especially from a normal procedure or standard.

> Those who **deviate** from the strict rules of the laboratory will not be allowed to retain their user identifications.

> Jose's fear of Maria's anger caused him to **deviate** from the truth.

(noun) A person who departs from the accepted norm or standard.

> Ming was considered a **deviate** by his neighbors because he refused to pay his taxes.

Synonyms: (verbs): veer, diverge, deflect, digress, swerve, wander, stray, ramble; (nouns): nonconformist, maverick, heretic, weirdo

Antonyms   (verbs): conform to, stick to, abide by, adhere to; (nouns): conformist, traditionalist, Mrs. Grundy

19. diligent (DILL uh junt) *adjective*

[Latin *diligens*, *diligentis*, esteeming highly; from *dis*, apart + *legere*, to choose]

Definition   Persistent in doing something; hardworking; constant and earnest in effort.

> Molly is so **diligent** at her job that she receives promotions regularly.

> Although I made a **diligent** search of my desk, I could not find the missing files.

Synonyms: active, industrious, laborious, persevering, attentive, untiring, careful

Antonyms: lazy, slothful, indolent, shiftless

SECOND GROUP: 11. boycott – 20. discourse (continued)

20. **discourse** (DIS kors) *noun;* (dis KORS) *verb*

[Latin *discursus,* conversation; from *dis,* in different directions + *currere, cursus,* run]

Definition   (noun) Exchange of thought by words; talk; a formal discussion.

Lisette wrote a lengthy **discourse** for her history class on the problems of becoming a U.S. citizen.

As the argument grew more heated, the **discourse** became less understandable.

(verb) To talk about or discuss at length.

In the company lunch room you can hear people **discoursing** about the state of the economy.

The editorial **discoursed** about the epidemic of mergers and acquisitions that has swept the business world.

Synonyms   (nouns): conversation, lecture, lesson, treatise, sermon, talk; (verbs): enlarge upon, expand on, reason

Antonyms   (these indicate brief, concise treatment): (nouns): summary, abstract, precis, synopsis; (verbs): summarize, outline, sketch

Let's take a few minutes for another workout with your ten additional words. Regular reviews help you more than anything else to gain quick word recognition and usage skills. Continue to build your vocabulary muscles and soon you will have a strong base of useful words.

Exercise #4 for Practice

Quick Check

Match each word in the first column with its definition in the second column. This exercise includes vocabulary words 11–20 and adds two words from exercise (1) for your review. Check your answers at the end of the section.

1. _____ adverse   a. turn aside

2. _____ augment   b. protest

3. _____ boycott   c. recurring

4. _____ cajole   d. permit

5. _____ candid   e. enlarge

6. _____ chronic   f. persistent

7. _____ cogent   g. convincing

8. _____ condone   h. talk

9. _____ copious   i. sincere

10. _____ deviate   j. plentiful

11. _____ diligent   k. unfavorable

12. _____ discourse   l. flatter

SECOND GROUP: 11. boycott – 20. discourse (continued)

Exercise #5 for Practice

Which Is Correct?

Choose the sentence (a, b, or c) that comes closest to describing each of the following situations. Check your answers at the end of the section.

1. Consumers occasionally **boycott** supermarkets when they are displeased with their products.

   ☐ a. Supermarkets take revenge on customers by locking their doors.

   ☐ b. Consumers join together and refuse to buy products they do not like from the supermarket.

   ☐ c. Products should meet customers' needs.

2. Jemimah **cajoled** her way into the concert by flirting with the gate attendant.

   ☐ a. The gate attendant thought Jemimah was cool.

   ☐ b. Jemimah flattered the gate attendant in order to see the concert for free.

   ☐ c. The concert was a special event and Jemimah had to find some way to attend.

3. Our manager, Frank Lee, speaks in such a **candid** manner that we always know exactly what he expects from us.

   ☐ a. Our manager tells us everything we need to know in an open, sincere style.

   ☐ b. Frank Lee trusts us.

   ☐ c. We must choose whether or not we should believe our manager.

4. The department secretary was a **chronic** complainer, which made working conditions difficult for the entire staff.

   ☐ a. The secretary played ''devil's advocate'' for the staff.

   ☐ b. The secretary hardly ever complained.

   ☐ c. The secretary complained a lot.

(continued)

Exercise #5 for Practice (continued)

5. Clarabelle's **cogent** speech convinced the agency to change its residency laws.

   ☐ a. Clarabelle argued so believably that the agency made the changes she suggested.

   ☐ b. The agency was about to change their requirements when Clarabelle spoke.

   ☐ c. If they did not change their residency requirements, Clarabelle would shut down the agency.

6. To ignore negative behavior is to **condone** it.

   ☐ a. Negative behavior is wrong.

   ☐ b. When you overlook bad behavior you are allowing it to continue.

   ☐ c. If you overlook negative behavior it will go away.

7. **Copious** stacks of mail awaited Rudolph when he returned from the conference.

   ☐ a. No one at the conference wrote to Rudolph.

   ☐ b. Rudolph did not have much mail.

   ☐ c. Rudolph found his in-basket full of mail.

8. Although the pilot must **deviate** from her flight plan because of the storm, we should still arrive at our destination on time.

   ☐ a. We should get to our meeting on time even though we must fly around the storm.

   ☐ b. The pilot does not know if she can get us to our meeting on time.

   ☐ c. We can go through the storm and get to our meeting on time.

(continued)

SECOND GROUP: 11. boycott – 20. discourse (continued)

Exercise #5 for Practice (continued)

9. Every member of the team made a **diligent** effort to meet the new budget deadline.

☐ a. The team did not take the deadline seriously.

☐ b. The team tried to meet the deadline, but gave up.

☐ c. The team worked especially hard to finish the budget on time.

10. After a heated **discourse,** management and the union reached an uneasy agreement.

☐ a. They agreed to disagree.

☐ b. Following an intense discussion they decided on a course of action.

☐ c. Management and the union reached agreement over a hot meal.

Exercise #6 for Practice

Yes or No—What's Your Guess?

Answer "Yes" or "No" to each of the following questions. Circle your answers. Check the end of the section for the correct response.

1. If you **boycott** a meeting, you attend it without fail.   Yes   No

2. To **cajole** someone is to persuade them with flattery.   Yes   No

3. **Candid** can only refer to a camera.   Yes   No

4. If you have a **chronic** illness, it develops slowly and becomes gradually more serious.   Yes   No

5. A **cogent** argument is convincing.   Yes   No

6. When you **condone** an action you stop it at all costs.   Yes   No

7. If you take **copious** notes, you are making a few scattered scribbles in the margin.   Yes   No

8. You **deviate** when you turn aside.   Yes   No

9. A **diligent** student goofs off constantly.   Yes   No

10. A **discourse** is a long talk.   Yes   No

THIRD GROUP: 21. docile – 30. inherent

21. docile (DOS ul) *adjective*

[Latin *docilis,* easily taught; from *docere,* to teach]

Definition   Easy to manage; easily taught; obedient.

> Baby raccoons appear **docile** at first, but later they may be impossible to control.

> Brent's employees were so **docile** that he was fooled into thinking they did not have minds of their own.

Synonyms: passive, latent, inert, torpid, submissive, willing

Antonyms: willful, strong minded, headstrong, perverse, stubborn

22. eminent (EM uh nunt) *adjective*

[Latin *eminens, eminentis,* standing out; from *ex,* out + *minere,* to project]

Definition   a. High in rank; renowned; exalted.

> The audience applauded wildly as the **eminent** musician completed a perfect piano recitation of a Mozart concerto.

b. Prominent or jutting; outstanding or conspicuous.

> Cherie could always find Franz in a crowd because of his **eminent** height.

Synonyms: notable, great, noteworthy, remarkable, famous, noted

Antonyms: obscure, lowly, unremarkable

23. ethical (ETH e kul) *adjective*

[Greek *ethikos,* moral; from *ethos,* custom]

Definition   Following the general principles of right conduct.

> Although Phineus did not accuse his insurance company of fraud, he wrote a letter to the Insurance Commission stating that the company's practices were not **ethical.**

Note: Ethics is a part of philosophy that addresses morals and moral choices of individuals. An *ethos* is the set of basic attitudes, beliefs, and values that make up a group or culture. Another word for ethos is *mores* (MOR ays), ''mind set.''

Synonyms: virtuous, honorable, decent, honest, correct, principled

Antonyms: lawless, unfair, unjust, immoral, dishonest, unprofessional

24. exploit (ek SPLOIT) *verb*; (EK sploit) *noun*

[Old French *exploit, explait,* to perform; from Latin *ex,* out of + *plicare,* fold]

Definition   (verb) To use for profit; to take advantage of.

> We must not continue to **exploit** our natural resources without replacing or renewing them or we will have nothing to leave for our children.

(noun) A heroic deed; an achievement.

> Waldo achieved a reputation as an exceptional pilot whose aerobatic **exploits** were known to everyone interested in airplanes.

Synonyms   (verbs): Make the most of, cash in on, improve, turn to profit, capitalize; (nouns): heroics, coup, tour de force, derring-do

25. flaunt (flawnt) *verb*

[Origin unknown; possibly from Swedish *flankt,* from *flanka,* to wave about; or from Norwegian *flanta,* to gad about]

Definition   To show off in a conspicuous or offensive way.

> Some lottery winners cannot handle sudden wealth, and they **flaunt** their money with outrageous displays of expensive purchases.
>
> ''If you've got it, **flaunt** it.''

Synonyms: wave, display, parade, exhibit, draw attention to

Antonyms: hide, conceal, deemphasize, cover up, down-play, cool it

26. foible (FOI bul) *noun*

[Old French, *feble,* weak]

Definition   A minor character flaw; a quirk in personality.

> The founder of the company has so many **foibles** that the board of directors asked him not to visit the headquarters building because he was upsetting the employees.
>
> Maggie's **foibles** included an obsession with germs.

Synonyms: frailty, defect, shortcoming, oddity

Antonyms: strength, forte, strong suit, talent

THIRD GROUP: 21. docile – 30. inherent (continued)

27. gullible (GUL uh bul) *adjective*

[English *gull,* to dupe + *ible*]

Definition   Easily deceived or cheated; naive.

Joey was always **gullible** to the tricks played on him by his office mates.

"Caveat emptor (Let the buyer beware)" is good advice for **gullible** shoppers.

Synonyms: artless, inexperienced, green, a soft touch, a sitting duck

Antonyms: skeptical, incredulous, doubtful, wary, cautious

28. heinous (HAY nus) *adjective*

[Old French *haineus,* hateful; from *hair,* to hate]

Definition   Utterly wicked or vile.

The army officer's act of treason was so **heinous** that the court recommended the death sentence.

Rape and murder are considered **heinous** crimes.

Synonyms: base, gross, odious, unforgivable, evil

Antonyms: commendable, admirable, honorable

29. impasse (IM pass) *noun*

[French *impasse,* dead end; from *in,* not + *passer,* pass]

Definition   A position from which there is no escape; a dead end.

The union negotiations reached an **impasse** at 2 A.M. and a strike was called.

When Mathilda reached an **impasse** with her boss, she requested a transfer to another department.

Synonyms: standstill, deadlock, blind alley, point of no return, a bind

30. inherent (in HARE unt) *adjective*

[Latin *inhaerens, inhaerentis,* sticking in; from *in,* in, + *haerere,* to stick]

Definition   Existing in someone or something as a natural quality or attribute.

> Noel possesses the **inherent** quality of kindness, and he treats everyone with gentleness and respect.

> An **inherent** belief in oneself is what causes most people to start their own businesses.

Synonyms: instinctive, intrinsic, implicit, internal, inner, built-in, organic, innate

Antonyms: extrinsic, external, outside, foreign, alien

Are your vocabulary muscles expanding? You are more than half-way through the vocabulary list. Keep up the good work!

NATURAL

THIRD GROUP: 21. docile – 30. inherent (continued)

Exercise #7 for Practice

Quick Check

This exercise includes vocabulary words 21–30 and adds five words from the previous lists for your review. Match each word in the first column with its definition in the second column. Check your answers at the end of the section.

1. _____	allege	a.	move away from
2. _____	avid	b.	take advantage of
3. _____	cajole	c.	eager
4. _____	cogent	d.	easily deceived
5. _____	deviate	e.	obedient
6. _____	docile	f.	flatter
7. _____	eminent	g.	monstrous
8. _____	ethical	h.	deadlock
9. _____	exploit	i.	assert
10. _____	flaunt	j.	persuasive
11. _____	foible	k.	quirk
12. _____	gullible	l.	acting correctly
13. _____	heinous	m.	built-in
14. _____	impasse	n.	show off
15. _____	inherent	o.	high ranking

Exercise #8 for Practice

Blankety Blanks

For each sentence below, choose the word that best completes its meaning. Check your answers at the end of the section.

1. Leviticus follows strong _____ principles that create a reputation of respect and trust among his associates.

    (a) benign (b) docile (c) gullible (d) heinous (e) ethical

2. When Suzie Q married a wealthy stockbroker, she began to _____ her new Jaguar and expensive jewels in front of her friends.

    (a) condone (b) flaunt (c) exploit (d) cajole (e) deviate

3. The new programmer had such a _____ nature that he never disturbed anyone or asked for special favors.

    (a) docile (b) diligent (c) candid (d) avid (e) gullible

4. Daisy Mae's manager began to _____ her singing talent and kept a large share of the profits for himself.

    (a) augment (b) boycott (c) condone (d) exploit (e) aggregate

5. Joaquin was so _____ that he continually gave away his money and possessions to anyone with a hard luck story.

    (a) adverse (b) astute (c) gullible (d) avid (e) chronic

6. Dr. Bone's _____ included wearing a mask and rubber gloves when talking to his patients on the telephone.

    (a) aggregate (b) foibles (c) discourse (d) boycott (e) deviate

7. The crime was so _____ that the police would not discuss the bloody details with the press.

    (a) heinous (b) chronic (c) benign (d) abject (e) candid

8. Professor Harrison's childhood in India gave him an _____ knowledge of the people's language and customs.

    (a) abject (b) askew (c) ethical (d) adverse (e) inherent

9. Our work team split up when we reached an _____ regarding the division of job responsibilities.

    (a) aggregate (b) exploit (c) impasse (d) adverse (e) eminent

10. The _____ author spoke with great authority about his experiences in Russia during the breakup of the republic.

    (a) gullible (b) avid (c) docile (d) eminent (e) heinous

THIRD GROUP: 21. docile – 30. inherent (continued)

Exercise #9 for Practice

How Are They Related?

For each vocabulary word below, decide whether the word opposite it in the second column is similar (S) in meaning, opposite (O) in meaning, or unrelated (U) in meaning. Check your answers at the end of the section.

1. _____ docile   obedient

2. _____ eminent   obscure

3. _____ ethical   immoral

4. _____ exploit   assert

5. _____ flaunt   show off

6. _____ foible   advantage

7. _____ gullible   naive

8. _____ heinous   admirable

9. _____ impasse   deadlock

10. _____ inherent   persuasive

FOURTH GROUP: 31. irony – 40. rescind

31. irony (IYE ron ee) *noun*

[Greek *eironeia*, feigning ignorance; from *eirein*, to speak]

Definition   A difference between what one might expect and what actually happens; a use of words to present a meaning that is the opposite of its real meaning.

> It is an **irony** that one of the world's richest men is declaring bankruptcy.

> ''I have the utmost respect for your work, George,'' Twyla stated with a sneer. The **irony** of her statement was that she was about to fire him.

Synonyms: contradiction, paradox, ambiguity

32. lucid (LOO sid) *adjective*

[Latin *lucidus*, clear; from *lucere*, to shine]

Definition   Clear; easy to understand.

> Although Herbert seldom spoke, his ideas were **lucid** and he explained them clearly with a few well-chosen words.

> When Granny Gritch died at the age of 90, she was **lucid** and her sense of humor was evident until the end.

Synonyms: crystal-clear, sane, rational, understandable, intelligible

Antonyms: confused, puzzling, insane, irrational

FOURTH GROUP: 31. irony – 40. rescind (continued)

33. novice (NOV us) *noun*

[French *novice;* from Latin *novicius,* a new member, from *novus,* new]

Definition   a.   A person who has just entered a religious order for a period of probation.

> Many **novices** find their first days in a religious community difficult, but they usually adjust to the sparse lifestyle fairly quickly.

b.   One who is new to the circumstances in which she or he has been placed; a beginner.

> When Terrance gave his first presentation in front of his staff he was such a **novice** that he continually tungled his tang.

Synonyms: trainee, rookie, greenhorn, tenderfoot, new kid on the block

Antonyms: expert, pro, veteran, old hand

34. paradox (PARE uh doks) *noun*

[Greek *paradoxos,* unbelievable; from *para,* beyond + *doxon,* opinion]

Definition   A seemingly contradictory remark that on closer examination expresses a possible truth.

> Oscar Wilde noted the **paradox** that there are two tragedies in life: one is not getting what you want; the other is getting it.

> Heinrich's job was a **paradox;** he was a wine taster who hated wine.

Synonyms: riddle, enigma, contradiction, dilemma, inconsistency

35. perjure (PUR jur) *verb*

[Latin *per*, harmfully + *jurare*, to swear]

Definition   To lie intentionally while under oath to tell the truth (as in a court of law).

> The defendant was convicted of bribery because later testimony revealed that she had **perjured** herself on the witness stand.

> Suzannah told the truth as tactfully as she could without actually **perjuring** herself.

Synonyms: swear falsely, prevaricate, lie, tell a whopper

36. premise (PREM is) *noun and verb*

[Latin *prae*, ahead + *mittere*, to send]

Definition   (noun) An assumption; the basis for a conclusion.

> Ziggy's department planned its yearly budget on the **premise** that sales would remain constant.

(verb) To take as the basis for a conclusion.

> Professor Raven **premised** his conclusion on the assumption that all human beings are created unequal.

Note: When used as a plural, **premises** also means a tract of land, including its buildings. ''The building inspector condemned the **premises** because the walls were unsafe.''

Synonyms   (nouns): antecedent, proposition, axiom, thesis, hypothesis; (verbs): preface, introduce, predicate, presuppose

FOURTH GROUP: 31. irony – 40. rescind (continued)

37. prolific (proh LIF ik) *adjective*

[Latin *proles,* offspring + *facere,* to make]

Definition   Highly productive; fruitful or fertile.

Beatrix was such a **prolific** writer that she finished three novels in one year.

The new equipment produced computer parts at a **prolific** rate.

Synonyms: profuse, effusive, gushing, teeming, productive, abundant

Antonyms: unproductive, sterile, barren, fruitless, empty

38. quell (kwel) *verb*

[Old English *cwellan,* to kill]

Definition   To crush, subdue, or cause to cease; to bring to an end, usually by force.

Management tried to **quell** fears of layoffs by holding group meetings to answer questions about the economy's effect on the business.

The police were unable to **quell** the riots in the ghetto because the gangs causing them were well organized.

Synonyms: suppress, crush, extinguish, stamp out, squelch, calm, allay

Antonyms: instigate, provoke, incite, kindle, enflame, arouse, stir up

39. raze (rayz) *verb*

[Latin *radere, rasus,* to scrape]

Definition   To level to the ground; tear down.

Work on our new administration building will begin as soon as the builders **raze** the old structure.

A tornado swept through the countryside and **razed** everything in its path.

Note: Do not confuse **raze** with *raise,* which means ''erect'' or ''build up,'' the opposite of what **raze** means.

Synonyms: flatten, demolish, obliterate

Antonyms: erect, raise, uplift, set up, build

40. rescind (ri SIND) *verb*

[Latin *re,* back + *scindere,* to cut]

Definition   To cancel or withdraw; to revoke or repeal.

Cleo sent a petition signed by everyone in the department asking management to **rescind** the unpopular new dress code.

When several people fainted, Clyde **rescinded** his order to work through lunch.

Synonyms: retract, recall, annul, delete, nullify, invalidate

Antonyms: confirm, enforce, endorse, uphold, ratify

By now you have mastered forty new words! These exercises will help you strengthen your new vocabulary even more.

FOURTH GROUP: 31. irony – 40. rescind (continued)

Exercise #10 for Practice

Quick Check

This exercise includes vocabulary words 31–40 and adds five words from previous lists. Match each word in the first column with its definition in the second column. Be patient with your progress, and check your answers at the end of the section.

1. _____ aggregate   a. a personality quirk

2. _____ astute   b. tear down

3. _____ candid   c. contradiction

4. _____ ethical   d. outspoken

5. _____ foible   e. to lie under oath

6. _____ irony   f. clear

7. _____ lucid   g. total of the parts

8. _____ novice   h. productive

9. _____ paradox   i. a beginner

10. _____ perjure   j. to subdue

11. _____ premise   k. keenly aware

12. _____ prolific   l. meaning the opposite

13. _____ quell   m. cancel

14. _____ raze   n. assumption

15. _____ rescind   o. acting correctly

Exercise #11 for Practice

Picky Pickies

Read the following statements, then pick the word that comes to mind. Circle your answer, then check your answers at the end of the section.

1. To calm a child's fears of the dark.
   (rescind,   quell,   raze)

2. To lie to a jury.
   (perjure,   irony,   rescind)

3. A dentist with bad teeth telling you to have regular checkups.
   (novice,   perjure,   irony)

4. Someone who is introduced to a computer for the first time.
   (novice,   lucid,   paradox)

5. To change your mind and cancel an order.
   (prolific,   premise,   rescind)

6. Thinking clearly.
   (irony,   lucid,   paradox)

7. To set fire to a field of sugar cane in order to clear it.
   (raze,   premise,   quell)

8. The hurrier I go the behinder I get.
   (prolific,   paradox,   rescind)

9. The national Constitution is founded on the idea that everyone is created equal.
   (premise,   rescind,   lucid)

10. Parents who have ten children.
    (raze,   novice,   prolific)

FOURTH GROUP: 31. irony – 40. rescind (continued)

Exercise #12 for Practice

T for True

In the spaces provided, indicate whether each statement below is true or false.

_____ 1. A snowstorm on the desert in July is an **irony.**

_____ 2. Legal documents are always **lucid.**

_____ 3. If you have worked on a job for twenty years you are a **novice.**

_____ 4. It is a **paradox** that someone outgoing can be very shy.

_____ 5. If you **perjure** yourself, that proves you are honest.

_____ 6. To argue a point reasonably, you must start with a valid **premise.**

_____ 7. Rabbits are said to be **prolific** because they have lots of babies.

_____ 8. One who **quells** a rumor is a gossip.

_____ 9. If you wish to **raze** a vacant lot you would start by building condos on it.

_____ 10. Management becomes unpopular when it **rescinds** benefits.

FIFTH GROUP: 41. ruse – 50. zenith

41. ruse (rooz) *noun*

[Old French *ruse,* a trick; from Latin *recusare,* to refuse]

Definition   A trick or strategy to confuse or mislead.

The secretaries used the **ruse** of a problem in the lab to get their manager out of the office while they planned her surprise birthday party.

The Trojan Horse was a **ruse** used by the Greeks to capture Troy.

Synonyms: ploy, plan, gimmick, scheme, bluff, dirty trick

42. salient (SAY lee unt); (SAYL yunt) *adjective*

[Latin *saliens, salientis,* jumping; from *salire,* to jump]

Definition   Prominent or conspicuous; standing out from the rest.

Elvira erupted angrily and made a few **salient** remarks to the receptionist as she left the office.

Lucas liked the **salient** angles of the new office complex in the architect's drawings.

Synonyms: outstanding, noticeable, striking, pronounced

Antonyms: inconspicuous, unobtrusive

43. schism (SIZZ um); (SKIZZ um) *noun*

[Greek *schisma,* a division; from *schizein,* to split]

Definition   A split or division within an organized group or society, especially within a religious group.

When elders in the synagog could not agree, there was a **schism** between liberals and conservatives.

During times of economic hardship, an ever widening **schism** occurs between the wealthy and the rest of society.

Synonyms: division, separation, breach, discord

Antonyms: union, aggregation, concord

FIFTH GROUP: 41. ruse – 50. zenith (continued)

44. secular (SEK yuh lur) *adjective*

[Latin *saecularis*, belonging to an age; from *saeculum*, an age]

Definition Not religious; pertaining to worldly rather than spiritual matters; affairs of the state.

At the concert, Anouk enjoyed a fine blend of sacred and **secular** music.

Many members of the clergy enjoy **secular** activities such as sailing, raising dogs and playing bridge.

Synonyms: ordinary, temporal, mundane, material, unsacred, worldly

Antonyms: sacred, holy, divine, spiritual, religious

45. strident (STRIDE ent) *adjective*

[Latin *stridens*, *stridentis*, loud; from *stridere*, to make a harsh noise]

Definition Loud, harsh, or grating.

The director's **strident** voice rang through the halls of the think tank, disrupting all who heard it.

The programmers were engaged in a **strident** disagreement over the design of the new screens.

Synonyms: grating, shrill, raucous, jarring, dissonant, angry

Antonyms: agreeable, melodious, harmonious, dulcet

46. tacit (TAS it) *adjective*

[Latin *tacitus*, silent; from *tacere*, to be silent]

Definition Implied or inferred; not spoken.

When the CEO returned my proposal without comment, I took this as **tacit** approval of my plan.

Teenagers share a **tacit** understanding of a vocabulary that eludes most adults.

Synonyms: understood, implicit, wordless, unexpressed

Antonyms: explicit, expressed, specific, defined

47. thwart (thwaart) *verb*

[Old Norse *thverr, thvert,* lying across]

Definition   To block or frustrate a plan.

Too much television can **thwart** children's interest in reading.

My plans to work late were **thwarted** by my son, who needed the car to go to football practice.

Synonyms: defeat, disappoint, frustrate, nip in the bud

Antonyms: help, promote, aid, advance

48. usurp (yoo SURP) *verb*

[Latin *usurpare,* to take possession of without legal claim; from *usu,* by use + *rapere,* to seize]

Definition   To seize and hold a position of power without the legal right to do so.

John tried to **usurp** the crown while his brother, King Richard, was away fighting for England.

The owner's scheming grandson **usurped** the position of manager in our department.

Synonyms: encroach, infringe, appropriate, assume, take command

49. vie (vye) *verb*

[Old French *envier,* to challenge; from Latin *invitare,* to invite]

Definition   To strive in competition or rivalry with another; to compete.

This year our department is sending a novice team to **vie** for the volleyball championship against ten other department teams in our organization.

Kim Lee and Giselle seem to **vie** constantly for our manager's attention.

Synonyms: contend against, tussle, come to blows

FIFTH GROUP: 41. ruse – 50. zenith (continued)

50. zenith (ZEE nuth) *noun*

[Old Spanish *zenit,* apex; from Arabic *semt ar-ras,* way of the head]

Definition   A point on the celestial sphere directly above a given position or an observer; the highest point.

At noon the sun is at its **zenith.**

The deadline grew closer, and we reached a **zenith** of activity as we struggled frantically to finish the project on time.

Synonyms: summit, apex, apogee, peak, height, acme, climax, pinnacle

Antonyms: nadir, perigee, rock bottom, lowest point

Congratulations! You have just mastered fifty new words. We hope you enjoy the new confidence you feel as you converse with your friends and business colleagues. To complete this chapter, work through the final Quick Check and review exercises.

Exercise #13 for Practice

Quick Check

Match each word in the first column with its definition in the second column. Then check your answers at the end of the section.

1. _____ abject		a.	trick
2. _____ docile		b.	deadlock
3. _____ impasse		c.	not religious
4. _____ perjure		d.	division
5. _____ quell		e.	implied
6. _____ ruse		f.	seize
7. _____ salient		g.	obedient
8. _____ schism		h.	compete
9. _____ secular		i.	swear falsely
10. _____ strident		j.	standing out
11. _____ tacit		k.	highest point
12. _____ thwart		l.	harsh
13. _____ usurp		m.	miserable
14. _____ vie		n.	block
15. _____ zenith		o.	suppress

Exercise #14 for Practice

Origins and Synonyms

From the origin [in brackets] and a synonym, fill in each blank with the correct word from the list. Check your answers at the end of the section.

ruse	salient	schism
secular	strident	tacit
thwart	usurp	vie
zenith		

1. [Greek *schizein*, to split]; *synonym:* breach _____

2. [Latin *stridere*, to make a harsh noise]; *synonym:* shrill _____

3. [Latin *usu*, by use + *rapere*, to seize]; *synonym:* take command

   _____

4. [Old Norse *thvert*, lying across]; *synonym:* defeat _____

5. [Latin *recusare*, to refuse]; *synonym:* ploy _____

6. [Latin *saeculum*, an age]; *synonym:* worldly _____

7. [Arabic *semt ar-ras*, way of the head]; *synonym:* height _____

8. [Latin *salire*, to jump]; *synonym:* pronounced _____

9. [Latin *invitare*, to invite]; *synonym:* contend against _____

10. [Latin *tacere*, to be silent]; *synonym:* wordless _____

FIFTH GROUP: 41. ruse – 50. zenith (continued)

Exercise #15 for Practice

Word Scramble

In the following exercise, rearrange the letters to spell each of the ten vocabulary words in this section. The words are in alphabetical order. After each word write a brief definition. Check your answers at the end of the section.

	Word	**Definition**
1. sure	_____	_____
		_____
2. lasenti	_____	_____
		_____
3. smisch	_____	_____
		_____
4. ceslaru	_____	_____
		_____
5. derstint	_____	_____
		_____
6. attic	_____	_____
		_____
7. whartt	_____	_____
		_____
8. pursu	_____	_____
		_____
9. ive	_____	_____
		_____
10. ezthin	_____	_____
		_____

ANSWERS TO SECTION 5 EXERCISES

EXERCISE #1

1. g; **2.** b; **3.** i; **4.** c; **5.** a; **6.** j; **7.** d; **8.** e; **9.** f; **10.** h

EXERCISE #2

1. askew; **2.** aggregate; **3.** astute; **4.** abject; **5.** augment; **6.** adverse; **7.** avid; **8.** allege; **9.** allude; **10.** benign

EXERCISE #3

1. dishonest; **2.** useful; **3.** trend; **4.** forfeit; **5.** avoid; **6.** awesome; **7.** stoic; **8.** endorse; **9.** inept; **10.** robust

EXERCISE #4

1. k; **2.** e; **3.** b; **4.** l; **5.** i; **6.** c; **7.** g; **8.** d; **9.** j; **10.** a; **11.** f; **12.** h

EXERCISE #5

1. b; **2.** b; **3.** a; **4.** c; **5.** a; **6.** b; **7.** c; **8.** a; **9.** c; **10.** b

EXERCISE #6

1. No; **2.** Yes; **3.** No; **4.** Yes; **5.** Yes; **6.** No; **7.** No; **8.** Yes; **9.** No; **10.** Yes

EXERCISE #7

1. i; **2.** c; **3.** f; **4.** j; **5.** a; **6.** e; **7.** o; **8.** l; **9.** b; **10.** n; **11.** k; **12.** d; **13.** g; **14.** h; **15.** m

EXERCISE #8

1. e; **2.** b; **3.** a; **4.** d; **5.** c; **6.** b; **7.** a; **8.** e; **9.** c; **10.** d

EXERCISE #9

1. S; **2.** O; **3.** O; **4.** U; **5.** S; **6.** U; **7.** S; **8.** O; **9.** S; **10.** U

ANSWERS TO SECTION 5 EXERCISES (continued)

EXERCISE #10

1. g; **2.** k; **3.** d; **4.** o; **5.** a; **6.** l; **7.** f; **8.** i; **9.** c; **10.** e; **11.** n; **12.** h; **13.** j; **14.** b; **15.** m

EXERCISE #11

1. quell; **2.** perjure; **3.** irony; **4.** novice; **5.** rescind; **6.** lucid; **7.** raze; **8.** paradox; **9.** premise; **10.** prolific

EXERCISE #12

1. T; **2.** F; **3.** F; **4.** T; **5.** F; **6.** T; **7.** T; **8.** F; **9.** F; **10.** T

EXERCISE #13

1. m; **2.** g; **3.** b; **4.** i; **5.** o; **6.** a; **7.** j; **8.** d; **9.** c; **10.** l; **11.** e; **12.** n; **13.** f; **14.** h; **15.** k

EXERCISE #14

1. schism; **2.** strident; **3.** usurp; **4.** thwart; **5.** ruse; **6.** secular; **7.** zenith; **8.** salient; **9.** vie; **10.** tacit

EXERCISE #15

1. ruse: trick; **2.** salient: standing out; **3.** schism: division **4.** secular: not religious; **5.** strident: harsh; **6.** tacit: implied; **7.** thwart: block; **8.** usurp: seize; **9.** vie: compete; **10.** zenith: highest point

SECTION

6

Idioms, Slang and Other Mutants

A DIFFERENT KIND OF GRAMMAR

Even if you hated grammar in school—or learned to say that you did—you will like this chapter. First, you will see how Standard English fits into our language. It is the cornerstone of American speech and worthy of our attention. However, you will discover that grammar rules and standard speech go only so far, then our language becomes quite unscientific. Ah, your suspicions are confirmed. For all of its claims of correctness, English is not very consistent. It is full of idioms, jargon, and slang—words that defy the rules and make sense only to those who use them. These "renegade" phrases make the language at once artistic, lovable and confusing. Idioms, jargon and slang are universally accepted and greatly affect our speaking and writing vocabularies.

If you want to build your vocabulary and understand English at its deepest level, become familiar with the information in this chapter. Your reward will be a tighter grasp of your speaking and writing style. You will develop a keener ability to make the right choice about what to say and how to say it. Use what you learn here. Ask, read, imitate and practice. Your goal is to have something to say, and to learn to say it well.

STANDARD ENGLISH

This is our language at its best and most formal. Standard English is the least offensive and most accepted form of spoken and written communication in our culture. It includes proper grammar (no "ain'ts" allowed), clear diction and correct usage. Most TV and radio newscasts are delivered in Standard English. Business letters and reports, speeches, magazines and textbooks are good examples. Standard English is a clear, descriptive language, with minimal slang or jargon. If you want to succeed in the United States you will have a much better chance if you master Standard English. Using substandard speech, including double negatives such as "I don't have no time," usually identifies the speaker as less educated and of a lower social standing than speakers who use English correctly.

The following description, by Robert Bone, of the island of Oahu in Hawaii, appears in his book *The Maverick Guide to Hawaii*. It is an example of Standard English.

> The gently sloping area between the Waianaes and the Koolaus traditionally has served as a wide agricultural belt, mostly composed of sugar and pineapple plantations. These green areas are still there, although there are examples of intruding urbanization now cutting into the fields.
>
> The shape of Oahu is so irregular, and its routes of commerce so winding, that standard compass directions are seldom used. Instead, today's population has maintained the ancient Hawaiian system of direction finding. There is *mauka* for inland or toward the mountains, and *makai* for toward the sea. Otherwise, the directions are indicated by naming known landmarks that lie farther along the same general path.

Everyone should know the guidelines for Standard English and should be able to use them effectively. You need them regularly when you present information to co-workers or management, write business documents, sell products, or talk with your superiors.

Remember that Standard English changes. Today it differs greatly from Shakespeare's English. If you were to speak Shakespearean English today, you would be considered weird—and probably unemployable.

One key element of speaking Standard English is pronouncing words correctly. Some people speak as though they had rented lips. Correct pronunciation means not only saying words properly, but also speaking your words clearly. If you speak correctly but sound as if you have a mouthful of raw broccoli, you are defeating your efforts.

WOUNDED WORDS

The following list of words is often mispronounced, because we hear them pronounced incorrectly so often that the wrong way sounds right. Be careful not to judge correct pronunciation as pretentious, or you limit yourself. There will always come a time when the correct pronunciation makes a difference to you. Read the correct pronunciations and, in the spaces below, check those that you routinely pronounce correctly. Then begin working on the others with the help of a friend.

	Word	Correct Pronunciation	Mispronunciation
1. _____	ask	ask	ax
2. _____	athlete	ATH leet	ATH uh leet
3. _____	burglar	BER gler	BER guh ler
4. _____	children	CHIL dren	CHIL dern
5. _____	column	COL um	COL yum
6. _____	creek	creek	crick
7. _____	directory	di REC tor ee	dir REC tree
8. _____	environment	en VI ron ment	en VI ern ment
9. _____	Arab	ARR ub	Ay rab
10. _____	February	FEB ru a ry	Feb u AIR ee
11. _____	genuine	JEN you in	jen you WINE
12. _____	height	hite	hite th
13. _____	hundred	HUN dred	HUN dert
14. _____	idea	i DEE uh	i DEER
15. _____	library	LIE brer ee	LIE bare ee
16. _____	nuclear	NEW clee ar	NEW que lar
17. _____	roof	roof	ruff
18. _____	silicon	sil i CON	sil i CONE
19. _____	sword	sord	sword
20. _____	yellow	YEL low	YEL ler

LAZY LIPS

Good speech is distinct. To speak clearly, remember the acronym LOMM—Large, Open, Moving Mouth. Motorize your jaw, engage your lips and ENUNCIATE. To practice separating words, write out what you think the following run-together sentences mean, then check the end of the section.

Exercise #1 for Practice

RUNTOGETHERSENTENCES

1. Dyaevr seeim? _____
2. Howvyabin? _____
3. Dyunnerstan? _____
4. Whachadoon? _____
5. I toljuhthousantimz. _____
5. I heardjuh. _____
7. Jeetchet? _____
8. I roetchalassmunt. _____
9. Woodjagimmesom? _____
10. Jawannadans? _____

Banishing Friction from Your Diction

The following words are often run together. Using LOMM, pronounce each word in the phrase slowly and distinctly until you can say it clearly. These exercises are especially useful if you use the telephone regularly, as you must speak more clearly in telephone communication.

and then	have to	for her	let me see	was he
an hour	idea of	for them	might have	would have
as yet	instead of	forget it	made of	get you
at all	some more	got it	put them	won't you
watch them	to go	give her	ought to	what did you do
would have	to hear	get him	saw her	how are you
going to	don't you	give me	should have	can't you
had to	need to	kept it	want to	

Syllables and Endings

The most important part of clear pronunciation is saying endings clearly. To pronounce final sounds distinctly, sound the final *ng* in words ending in *-ing*: *thinking, helping;* not *thinkin'* or *helpin'*. Pronounce the final letters of words ending in consonants: *would,* not *wou';* and sound the voiced syllables within words: *probably,* not *prolly.*

Say This	Not This
enjoyiNG	enjoyin'
trippiNG	trippin'
worlD	worl'
righT	righ'
builD, builT	buil'
inspecT	inspec'
drafT	draf'
recommenD	recommen'
amounT	amoun'
enTertaiNment	en'ertai'ment
inTeresting	in'erestin'
bAlloon	b'loon
breaDth	brea'th

Tongue Twisters

Repeat the following tongue twisters until you can say them easily. Begin slowly and move those lips. Number 5 is considered to be the most difficult sentence in the English language.

1. A tree toad loved a she-toad that lived up in a tree. She was a three-toed tree toad, but a two-toed toad was he.

2. A basket of biscuits, a basket of mixed biscuits, a basket of biscuit mixes.

3. Sixty-two sick chicks sat on six slim, slick, slender saplings.

4. Great rats, small rats, lean rats, brawny rats, brown rats, black rats, gray rats, tawny rats.

5. The sixth sheik's sixth sheep's sick.

A WORD ABOUT ACCENTS

Do not worry about accents. They are interesting and most people listen better to speakers with accents. However, if your accent is very strong, consider an accent-reduction class. If you cannot be understood when you speak, then Standard English will not matter anyway.

Sometimes self-consciousness about accents causes people to speak softly; so the listener must contend with both volume and accent. Try to speak loudly enough to be heard without straining. Speak at a moderate rate of speed, with energy in your voice.

When you do not understand someone because of an accent, stop him or her and ask politely if they will please repeat what they said. It is better that either of you be a bit embarrassed, than for you to misunderstand his or her meaning. And yes, if you still do not understand after a second attempt, ask a third time, even more politely.

Now that you have become familiar with Standard English, let's look at the outlaw elements of our language that are not so predictable. Idioms, jargon and slang add interest and complexity to English. These words and phrases make our language unique.

IDIOMS

In English, we hear and use idioms often. Whenever you hear a phrase whose meaning you cannot understand, even if you know the meaning of each separate word, you have probably run into an idiom. Examples of idioms include: *run into* (encounter; meet); *fly off the handle* (become angry). We cannot ignore idioms because the English language contains thousands of them. Instead we should learn to understand them and use them easily.

Idioms, along with slang, are considered part of everyday informal speech that is understood by most Americans, regardless of their education. Twenty of the most common idioms and their definitions are listed below. A practice exercise follows.

Idiom	Definition
1. tighten your belt	economize, spend less money
2. on pins and needles	nervous or excited
3. an arm and a leg	a large amount of money
4. in a pinch	when nothing else is available
5. nest egg	money set aside or saved
6. face up to	accept something unpleasant or difficult
7. one for the books	something unusual or unexpected
8. a drop in the bucket	a small amount
9. bring home the bacon	earn the family income
10. under the weather	not feeling well
11. pitch in	help
12. eager beaver	ambitious, hard worker
13. well-heeled	rich
14. out of the blue	unexpectedly
15. shape up	start to act or look right
16. in seventh heaven	very happy
17. means business	is very serious about something
18. keep your fingers crossed	wish for good luck
19. jump the gun	start too soon
20. the cream of the crop	the best

PRACTICING IDIOMS

Complete the sentences with the correct idiom from the previous list. Check your answers at the end of the section.

Exercise #2 for Practice

1. The extra money was a big surprise. It came _____.
2. These numbers might win the lottery. _____ for good luck.
3. Dong Chou saved a large _____ to buy a house someday.
4. A flu epidemic hit our office staff and everyone is _____.
5. _____, you can substitute overhead transparencies for handouts.
6. The bid on the project was so close that the sales team was _____ until they heard the results.
7. Maria was _____ when she heard about her promotion.
8. Our manager is _____, as he inherited $500,000 from his father's estate.
9. If we all _____, we can finish by noon.
10. During a recession you have to _____ and watch your budget carefully.
11. Franz always tries to finish his work before everyone else. He is an _____.
12. We chose the prettiest, best behaved puppy. She was certainly _____.
13. If Madge doesn't _____, she could lose her job.
14. Our new office was very expensive. It cost _____.
15. The IRS audit was extremely thorough. They actually owe us money, which is _____.
16. Don't _____ and pay the bill before it is due.
17. Isabelle finally had to _____ her co-workers' accusations.
18. In today's economy, both husband and wife must _____ in order to meet their financial obligations.
19. When our manager says we have to complete the report by Friday, ''or else,'' I think she _____.
20. Sigmund's donation to charity was _____ compared to what was needed.

JARGON

Jargon, also called shoptalk, is the specialized vocabulary within a profession. Workers in various occupations use words familiar to themselves but meaningless to anyone else. Jargon has value because it unites people in their professions by allowing them to share a common vocabulary. It creates a feeling of uniqueness and provides a sense of protection from the outside world. Newcomers must ''break the code'' and learn the jargon before they are accepted into the group. Following are examples of jargon from different professions.

Jargon	Translation
Law	
lien \leen\	property held as security against debt
perjury	lying under oath
deposition	testimony taken down in writing under oath
embezzle	to steal money entrusted to your care
larceny	theft
Computers	
binary	number system on which computer operations are based, using only the numbers 0 and 1
chip	small modules of silicon that are the building blocks of computers
database	a collection of information manipulated by the computer
hard disk	a permanent, rigid computer storage medium
modem	a device that allows computers to communicate with each other
Business	
bottom line	final figures on a profit-and-loss statement
CEO	chief executive officer (top dog)
ROI	return on investment; what you get back for what you put in
downsizing	reducing employees and inventory in an organization in order to reduce cost
nonexempt	employees who are paid by the hour

Practicing with Jargon

List ten words or phrases from your occupation that you consider to be jargon. Remember that these terms may exclude people who are not involved in your kind of work. Use them appropriately.

_____   _____

_____   _____

_____   _____

_____   _____

_____   _____

SLANG

Slang does not fill a void in our vocabulary, in fact, it often provides new terms even where none are needed. Slang is not a part of our standard speech. It is entertainment, another way to say something, a shortcut to the mind. In any language slang is a proving ground for new words. New words are not brought by the stork. Rather, they enter a language because they are useful and expressive. ''In-groups'' and their code words merge with regular vocabulary, and over time, slang finds its way into our dictionaries. Slang can be the select speech of groups who wish to be different. Although slang creates group identity, it is not necessarily job related. Slang is a badge of membership among such groups as teenagers, Hell's Angels, and jazz musicians, to name a few. Only those who belong to the group can make sense of its particular slang.

Much slang consists of clever or insulting nicknames for types of people: *nerds, wimps, dweebs.* Social taboos are targets for slang as well: *barf, cow chips, blimp out.* Slang is a part of all cultures. Most slang lasts only a few years, then disappears. However, some imaginative words that begin as slang eventually become respectable words in the language, such as *joke, fad, boom, crank, slump.* Probably 35,000 expressions have come and gone in American slang. Slang is as much a part of America as blue jeans and the local mall.

Should you use slang? By all means, yes. In fact, you would have a hard time avoiding it. As an experiment, hold a conversation with a friend and avoid all idioms (see previous section) and slang. *It's the pits* to converse without using slang. With your friends, at parties, and in casual conversations, slang adds color and energy to your communications. Be careful not to overuse it, however, and select your words carefully. Some slang is *totally gross.* Some is overused and boring. And sometimes we use slang as a poor substitute for deeper thinking. Nothing dates us faster than old slang. At various times, *mercy, pshaw, heavy* and *movie* were ''in'' slang.

Use slang on the job carefully. When you start a new job, listen more than you talk for the first few weeks. How much slang do co-workers use and what kind is it? Then ''go native'' and begin using *their* words, at least the ones you are comfortable with. You will find yourself fitting in faster and more easily when you take your cue from others.

Twenty slang words and phrases, their definitions, and sentences using the slang terms are listed below.

	Slang	Definition	Sentence
1.	crash and burn	to fail miserably at something	I crashed and burned on my accounting exam.
2.	dude	a male friend; a guy	Hey dude! What's happenin'?
3.	flake out	back out of; fall asleep	Hal flaked out of the meeting.
4.	jock	an athlete	All of the jocks live in one dorm.
5.	jazzed	alert; excited; positive	Zena is jazzed about her vacation.
6.	schmooze	chat or gossip	Let's schmooze during coffee break.
7.	chill out	calm down; be quiet	Everyone chill out so we can discuss the problem rationally.
8.	burbs	suburbs	Hallie commutes 40 miles from the burbs every day.
9.	catch some Zs	sleep	Ryan tried to catch some Zs before the exam.
10.	el cheapo	the least expensive one	My second car is an el cheapo.
11.	rad	great; wonderful	What a rad suit!
12.	steamed	angry	Harry was steamed at his insurance company.
13.	hit the bricks	start walking	Agree to our demands or we hit the bricks.
14.	freak (out)	to be shocked or disoriented	Everyone freaked when the earthquake hit.
15.	freebie	something given for free	The ski tickets were freebies from the manager.
16.	maxed out	exhausted; tired	Felix has been working too hard and he is maxed out.
17.	shades	dark glasses	I need my shades. The sun is too bright.
18.	gofer	Someone who goes for things and brings them back; an underling	Barry was hired as a gofer to pick up documents from headquarters.
19.	nuts	crazy	The noisy fan is driving me nuts.
20.	quick fix	a fast, though temporary, solution	We did a quick fix on the circuit-board assembler.

SLANG (continued)

Exercise #3 for Practice

Practicing with Slang

Match the slang terms from the list on the previous page with the following definitions. There are twenty slang terms and ten sentences, so you will not use all of the terms listed above. Check your answers at the end of the section.

1. Stella was so _____ that she slept through the seminar.

2. Jake is such a _____ that he spends all of his time at the gym.

3. You are _____ to walk in the alley after midnight.

4. If you will _____ I'll explain everything.

5. Ashley really _____ when he heard the bad news.

6. Ziggy and Rick are real talkers and _____ at every opportunity.

7. Our family moved to the _____ to get away from the city traffic.

8. Do not spend too much money for tickets. Get the _____ seats.

9. Can you do a _____ on the engine to keep it running for a few days?

10. You look tired. Why don't you _____ on the coach?

HEADS UP

The information in this chapter is not new news. No matter what work you do, whether you are a student, a computer analyst, an assembly line worker, or a hospital administrator, others will judge you by the way you speak (and what you wear). Everyone agrees that these evaluations are unfair, but it is the way of the world. Choose how you want others to evaluate you and meet that standard. You are in charge. Speak effectively and dress for the job you want, not the job you have.

ANSWERS TO SECTION 6 EXERCISES

EXERCISE #1

1. Do you ever see him? **2.** How have you been? **3.** Do you understand?
4. What are you doing? **5.** I told you a thousand times. **6.** I heard you.
7. Did you eat yet? **8.** I wrote to you last month. **9.** Would you give me some?
10. Do you want to dance?

EXERCISE #2

1. out of the blue; **2.** Keep your fingers crossed; **3.** nest egg; **4.** under the
weather; **5.** in a pinch; **6.** on pins and needles; **7.** in seventh heaven;
8. well-heeled; **9.** pitch in; **10.** tighten your belt; **11.** eager beaver; **12.** the
cream of the crop; **13.** shape up; **14.** an arm and a leg; **15.** one for the
books; **16.** jump the gun; **17.** face up to; **18.** bring home the bacon;
19. means business; **20.** a drop in the bucket

EXERCISE #3

1. maxed out; **2.** jock; **3.** nuts; **4.** chill out; **5.** freaked; **6.** schmooze; **7.** burbs;
8. el cheapo; **9.** quick fix; **10.** catch some Zs

S E C T I O N

7

Odd Words, Puzzles and Games

LET'S HAVE FUN!

Vocabulary study should be fun. You can think of the English language either as a gallery of linguistic horrors or as a playground for the curious mind. If you enjoy the antics of semantics, this section provides a variety of odd words, puzzles, and games to increase your enthusiasm. The following poem by Richard Lederer, from his book *Crazy English,* is a good example of the curiosity of our language. He shows how verb tenses can make us tense.

The verbs in English are a fright.
How can we learn to read and write?
Today we speak, but first we spoke;
Some faucets leak, but never loke.
Today we write, but first we wrote;
We bite our tongues, but never bote.

Each day I teach, for years I taught,
And preachers preach, but never praught.
This tale I tell; this tale I told;
I smell the flowers, but never smold.

If knights still slay, as once they slew,
Then do we play, as once we plew?
If I still do as once I did,
Then do cows moo, as they once mid? . . .

About these verbs I sit and think.
These verbs don't fit. They seem to wink
At me, who sat for years and thought
Of verbs that never fat or wought.

ODD WORDS

Don't Give In to *Take*

Although it is a common word, *take* is a weak verb that conveys little information. In formal English and business writing avoid the verb *take* when you mean *attend, require, accept, need,* or *be necessary.*

Exercise #1 for Practice

How can the following sentences be improved? Rewrite the sentences substituting one of the verbs listed above for the word *take,* then check your answers at the end of the section.

1. Thinking takes brains.

   _____

2. I take evening classes at our local community college.

   _____

3. Do you take Visa or Mastercard?

   _____

4. Miko always does what it takes to get the job done.

   _____

5. It takes money to start a new business.

   _____

Precision Pays

You can use your present vocabulary to describe a person or a situation more accurately. Brighten your language with precise words that say what you mean.

Exercise #2 for Practice

Perhaps someone is not really *funny*, but comical, amusing, artistic, entertaining, clever, jolly, playful, joyful or outrageous. Which of these adjectives meaning the same as *funny* can be used to describe the people in the following list? Check your answers at the end of the section.

1. Bob Hope _____
2. a circus clown _____
3. a puppy _____
4. a magician _____
5. a child at Christmas _____
6. Santa Claus _____
7. a practical joker _____

Exercise #3 for Practice

Perhaps a person is not really *smart*, but intellectual, clever, bright, quick witted, crafty, brilliant, resourceful, original, studious, creative, shrewd, or wise. Which adjectives meaning the same as *smart* can be used to describe each person in the following list? Check your answers at the end of the section.

1. Einstein _____
2. Picasso _____
3. a straight A student _____
4. an inventor _____
5. Shakespeare _____
6. street-smart teenagers _____
7. a wealthy executive _____

ODD WORDS (continued)

Exercise #4 for Practice

Puzzling Vocabulary

Listed below are twenty vocabulary words from Section 5. In the box of letters, reading up, down, across, or diagonally, you will find twelve of the twenty words. As you locate each one, draw a circle around it as in the example. Then check your answers at the end of the section.

allude	condone	lucid	tacit
abject	docile	novice	thwart
avid	eminent	raze	usurp
benign	flaunt	ruse	vie
cajole	irony	strident	zenith

S	A	Z	T	A	C	I	T
T	V	B	D	A	R	V	C
R	I	X	J	O	H	I	O
I	D	O	N	E	G	E	N
D	L	Y	L	U	C	I	D
E	M	I	N	E	N	T	O
N	E	B	E	N	I	G	N
T	H	W	A	R	T	F	E

Daffynition

Lining A bright flash of light. *We ran for cover when we heard the thunder and saw the lining.*

Vary Very

Avoid the word *very*. It seldom adds meaning, and you can usually find a better adjective. A very big building is massive, towering, or grand. A very active child is more accurately lively or curious; very lazy is indolent, and very sure is positive.

Exercise #5 for Practice

In the following phrases, eliminate the word *very* and find two adjectives to express each phrase. Use your thesaurus if necessary. Check your answers at the end of the section.

1. Very rich _____ or _____
2. Very poor _____ or _____
3. Very tired _____ or _____
4. Very unusual _____ or _____
5. Very neat _____ or _____

Getting Rid of *Get*

Get is probably the most overused verb in the English language. Of course it is also useful, especially in idiomatic language such as "getting by," "getting ahead," or "getting around." In these phrases it is useful and adds color and energy to language. However, *get* is usually a symptom of laziness, and a better word is likely to be lurking nearby. Instead of saying "Please get a chair," say "Please bring a chair." In formal English and in writing, avoid *get* when possible. When you do use *get*, be sure to say *get* rather than *git*.

ODD WORDS (continued)

Exercise #6 for Practice

Rewrite the following sentences, substituting a more descriptive verb for the word *get*. Check your answers at the end of the section.

1. They cannot get the parts to us next week.

   _____

2. Augusta gets $500 a week in commissions.

   _____

3. Can we get them to meet our deadline?

   _____

4. If you want to get rich, work hard.

   _____

5. Mina got ill while working in the chemical laboratory.

   _____

6. Tom and Louise were eager to get to the conference.

   _____

7. If we can get the equipment soon, we can begin.

   _____

8. Our team hopes to get an award for our design.

   _____

9. Bingo got thrown out of his apartment.

   _____

10. When you pay attention, you get what is being said.

    _____

Portmanteau Words

A portmanteau (port MAN toe) word, sometimes called a blend, is a combining of two words into one. For example, *brunch* is a combination of *breakfast* and *lunch*. Other examples are listed below.

Exercise #7 for Practice

Next to each word, write the words that are combined to form the portmanteau word. Check your answers at the end of the section.

1. flurry _____ and _____

2. splatter _____ and _____

3. simulcast _____ and _____

4. smog _____ and _____

5. motel _____ and _____

6. guesstimate _____ and _____

7. sitcom _____ and _____

8. hassle _____ and _____

Daffynition

Money The day after Sunny. *We get paid next Money.*

NEOWORDS

Our language grows and changes whether we approve or not. Some neowords (new words) are elegant; some are uninhibited by good taste. New words are responses to our demands for expression. As such, they reflect our society's changes and attitudes. When words are useful they remain in the language, and when they outlive their usefulness they disappear. As Harry Homa told his high school English class in the Bronx, "Some words fly, and some words die." Listed below are twelve new words and definitions that have come into the English language in the past ten years. These words are new enough that they may not be encoded in your word processor's spelling checker. For other neowords, see an up-to-date dictionary.

Arablish, Frenglish, Spanglish, Japanglish *noun and adjective* Arabic, French, Spanish, or Japanese laced with English. These are portmanteau words showing the global mixing of modern languages.

biochip *noun* Another portmanteau word combining *bio*, meaning "life," and *chip*, as in "silicon chip." It means a computer chip that relies on organic materials or proteins and enzymes to send signals. This chip is an experiment that aims at producing faster computers than is possible with chips that send electronic signals.

caller ID *noun* A telephone service that flashes the caller's telephone number on a small screen.

cyberphobia *noun* The mental state of someone who is intimidated by computers.

hot button *noun* Highly charged feelings about a personal issue.

infobit *noun* A single item of information that meets the requirements for inclusion in a computer database.

loose cannon *noun* A person whose careless or reckless behavior endangers other people.

politicide *noun* Another portmanteau word, meaning "political suicide." Loss of power in politics by compromising on campaign promises.

proactive *adjective* Attempting to control events by taking an active part in making them happen.

seasonal affective disorder *noun* A state of depression caused by short winter days and lack of sun. Relieved by the arrival of spring.

tin parachute *noun* Salary and benefits guaranteed to a worker as a result of a dismissal during a merger or hostile takeover.

workquake *noun* An upheaval in the way employees work, often the result of computerization.

List as many neowords as you can think of on the lines below. Note whether they are jargon, old words with new meanings, or portmanteau words. Check a current dictionary to see if they are listed. Watch them over the next few years to see if they "fly or die."

_____   _____

_____   _____

_____   _____

_____   _____

_____   _____

_____   _____

Daffynition

Neck store Adjacent. *You can get them at the place neck store.*

ABBREVIATIONS

Here is a list of helpful abbreviations with correct capitalization and punctuation. Review them, then check your memory by completing the quiz that follows.

assn.	Association	km	kilometer(s)
assoc.	Associates	MC	master of ceremonies
asst.	assistant	MD	medical doctor
attn.	attention	MIA	missing in action
aux.	auxiliary	MVP	most valuable player
AWOL	absent without leave	PS	[Latin *postscriptum*] postscript
C	celsius, centigrade	PC	personal computer
c/o	in care of	PhD	doctor of philosophy
Co.	Company	POW	prisoner of war
Corp.	Corporation	R & D	research and development
CRT	cathode ray tube	RAM	random-access memory
db	decibels	ROM	read-only memory
dept.	department	RSVP	[French *répondez s'il vous plaît*] please reply
DOA	dead on arrival	SWAK	sealed with a kiss
ETA	estimated time of arrival	TKO	technical knockout
etc.	[Latin *et cetera*] and so on	TLC	tender loving care
F	Fahrenheit	UFO	unidentified flying object
FYI	for your information	VCR	video cassette recorder
govt.	government	VIP	very important person
i.e.	[Latin *id est*] that is	w/	with
Inc.	Incorporated	w/o	without
K	[Greek *chilioi*] thousand		

Exercise #8 for Practice

Activate your RAM, cover the definitions above and identify the following abbreviations for practice. Check your answers when you are finished.

1. TKO _____
2. asst. _____
3. CRT _____
4. PC _____
5. RAM _____
6. aux. _____
7. Corp. _____
8. w/o _____
9. RSVP _____
10. km _____
11. FYI _____
12. PhD _____
13. attn. _____
14. c/o _____
15. SWAK _____

ANSWERS TO SECTION 7 EXERCISES

EXERCISE #1

1. Thinking requires brains. **2.** I attend evening classes at our local community college. **3.** Do you accept Visa or Mastercard? **4.** Miko always does what is necessary to finish the job. **5.** You need money to start a new business.

EXERCISE #2

1. entertaining; **2.** comical; **3.** playful; **4.** clever; **5.** joyful; **6.** jolly;
7. outrageous

EXERCISE #3

1. brilliant; **2.** creative; **3.** studious; **4.** original; **5.** wise; **6.** quick witted;
7. shrewd

EXERCISE #4

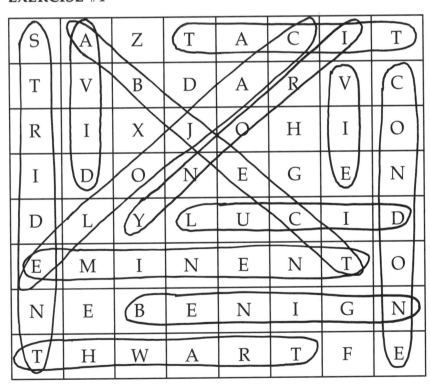

EXERCISE #5

Possible answers (there are many others): **1.** wealthy or affluent; **2.** broke or penniless; **3.** exhausted or weary; **4.** unique or outstanding; **5.** tidy or orderly

EXERCISE #6

1. They can't send the parts to us until next week. **2.** Augusta earns $500 a week in commissions. **3.** Can we persuade them to meet our deadline? **4.** If you want to grow rich, work hard. **5.** Mina became ill while working in the chemical laboratory. **6.** Tom and Louise were eager to arrive at the conference. **7.** If we can purchase the equipment soon, we can begin. **8.** Our team hopes to win an award for our design. **9.** Bingo was evicted from his apartment. **10.** When you pay attention, you understand what is being said.

EXERCISE #7

1. flutter and hurry; **2.** splash and spatter; **3.** simultaneous and broadcast; **4.** smoke and fog; **5.** motor and hotel; **6.** guess and estimate; **7.** situation and comedy; **8.** haggle and tussle

DEVELOPING A PERSONAL ACTION PLAN

A definition of *accountability* is ''responsibility for one's actions.''

We all have good intentions. The thing that separates those who are successful from those who are not is how well these good intentions are carried out.

A voluntary action plan can convert your good intentions into actions.

The PERSONAL ACTION PLAN on the next page is a good starting point if you are serious about improving your vocabulary skills.

You can act on your action plan any time you are reading, speaking, or listening (which is most of the time).

PERSONAL ACTION PLAN

Think about the information you have read in this book. Review the exercises. What did you learn about building a good vocabulary? What did you learn about your vocabulary skills? How can you improve your word power? Make a commitment to improving your vocabulary in your business and personal life. Design a personal action plan to help you reach your goal.

The following guide will help you clarify your goals and outline actions to achieve them.

1. My current vocabulary skills are effective in the following areas:

   _____

   _____

2. I need to improve my vocabulary skills in the following areas:

   _____

   _____

3. I will implement an action plan for vocabulary improvement in the following manner:

   A. My goals for building my vocabulary (be specific):

   _____

   _____

   _____

   B. My plan for reaching my goals:

   _____

   _____

   _____

   C. My timetable:

   _____

   _____

   _____

4. The following person(s) will benefit from my improved vocabulary:

   _____

5. They will benefit in the following ways:

   _____

   _____

NOTES

NOTES

NOTES

NOTES

NOTES

NOTES

OVER 150 BOOKS AND 35 VIDEOS AVAILABLE IN THE 50-MINUTE SERIES

We hope you enjoyed this book. If so, we have good news for you. This title is part of the best-selling *50-MINUTE*™ *Series* of books. All *Series* books are similar in size and identical in price. Many are supported with training videos.

To order *50-MINUTE* Books and Videos or request a free catalog, contact your local distributor or Crisp Publications, Inc., 1200 Hamilton Court, Menlo Park, CA 94025. Our toll-free number is (800) 442-7477.

50-Minute Series Books and Videos Subject Areas . . .

Management
Training
Human Resources
Customer Service and Sales Training
Communications
Small Business and Financial Planning
Creativity
Personal Development
Wellness
Adult Literacy and Learning
Career, Retirement and Life Planning

Other titles available from Crisp Publications in these categories

Crisp Computer Series
The Crisp Small Business & Entrepreneurship Series
Quick Read Series
Management
Personal Development
Retirement Planning